Sex

A Philosophical Primer

Books by Irving Singer

Sex: A Philosophical Primer

*Feeling and Imagination: The Vibrant Flux
of Our Existence*

Explorations in Love and Sex (forthcoming)

George Santayana, Literary Philosopher

Reality Transformed: Film as Meaning and Technique

*Meaning in Life:
The Creation of Value
The Pursuit of Love
The Harmony of Nature and Spirit*

*The Nature of Love:
Plato to Luther
Courtly and Romantic
The Modern World*

*Mozart and Beethoven: The Concept of Love
in Their Operas*

The Goals of Human Sexuality

Santayana's Aesthetics

Essays in Literary Criticism by George Santayana (editor)

*The Nature and Pursuit of Love: The Philosophy of
Irving Singer* (edited by David Goicoechea)

Sex

A Philosophical Primer

Irving Singer

ROWMAN & LITTLEFIELD PUBLISHERS, INC.
Lanham • Boulder • New York • London

ROWMAN & LITTLEFIELD PUBLISHERS, INC.

Published in the United States of America
by Rowman & Littlefield Publishers, Inc.
4720 Boston Way, Lanham, Maryland 20706
www.rowmanlittlefield.com

12 Hid's Copse Road
Cumnor Hill, Oxford OX2 9JJ, England

British Library Cataloguing in Publication Information Available

Library of Congress Cataloging-in-Publication Data

Singer, Irving.
    Sex : a philosophical primer / Irving Singer.
      p. cm.
    Includes bibliographical references and index.
    ISBN 0-7425-1236-3 (cloth : alk. paper)
      1. Sex—Philosophy. I. Title.

  B945.S6573 S49 2001
  128'.3—dc21
                                            00-065324

Printed in the United States of America

∞™ The paper used in this publication meets the minimum
requirements of American National Standard for Information
Sciences—Permanence of Paper for Printed Library Materials,
ANSI/NISO Z39.48-1992.

To Felipe and Reyes

Contents

Preface

This book is a philosophical primer in two respects. It explores elemental principles in the study of sex, and it addresses readers who are not trained philosophers as well as those who are. While being an inquiry into the sexuality of our species, the book does not attempt to deal with all the intriguing issues that cluster about that aspect of life.

If we compare the end of the twentieth century with its beginning, we are struck by the liveliness of questioning in this area that has now arisen as never before. Though I will be engaging only a few of the multiple queries, I recognize the importance of others that I bypass in my line of reasoning. Thanks to the fact that women, in particular, have found their own voice in matters related to sex, innovative work currently being done in gender studies augurs well for the future. Writings that derive from recent psychoanalytic, sexological, and socially oriented points of view have also made steady and cumulative progress.[1] In a more piecemeal fashion, technical philosophers are finally offering their type of sophistication.[2] Albeit selective and mainly panoramic from its own perspective, my book tries to contribute to the philosophical approach while also addressing relevant questions that readers of every sort may have in common. These are questions that focus upon the nature of sex and its valuation. They are supplemental to the others in this field, and may possibly underlie them.

In the first chapter I locate sex within a spectrum that includes love and compassion as well. Since compassion is a form of love, my belief that these three are inherently interwoven is principally directed toward clarifying the inner relations between sex and one or another type of love. I conclude that significant mistakes have persistently occurred because many theorists relegated sex, love, and compassion to separate and distinct compartments. These thinkers, and ordinary people influenced by them, failed to realize that our affective dispositions cannot be understood apart from the ways in which they interact with each other.

My emphasis upon the internal linkage between sex and the varieties of love is further elaborated in later portions of the book. In the second chapter I revert to an earlier distinction of mine, now somewhat revised and refurbished, between what I call "the sensuous" and "the passionate" as two components in sexual experience or behavior. I point out that both can belong to an attitude of love, and I speculate about the possibility of their harmonious combination. At the same time I probe the origins and the implications of the mutual hostility between them that has so often prevented any viable harmonization.

The distinction between the sensuous and the passionate serves as an entry into the ideas about the nature and valuation of sex that I propose in the third chapter. There I discuss how sex is both an appetite and an interpersonal drive. I claim that much philosophical confusion has resulted from the doctrines of those who constrain sexuality within either drive to the detriment of the other. I argue that what is sexual for human beings is normally, and perhaps always in some degree, a composite of the appetitive and the interpersonal. The former is the product of biological roots and the latter manifests a social need for intimate contact and corroboration of one's being. The mingling of these major components is distinctively human. In us sex is generically a function of both.

This conception of appetitive and interpersonal strands as unified in our sexuality is crucial for understanding the value of individual sex acts as well as their basic constitution. In the fourth chapter that outlook becomes the theme of my reflections about what can reasonably count as criteria of sexual goodness. My discussion is organized in terms of the following candidates: pleasure, enjoyment, satisfaction, completeness, reciprocity, love, embodiment, absorption, and the "natural" (as opposed to the "unnatural").

Since these possible criteria pertain to intrinsic rather than ethical goodness, the fifth chapter examines questions about sex as an aesthetic phenomenon. Can there be an *art* of sex, comparable to the arts of music, poetry, sculpture, or even cooking and rug weaving? I concentrate upon the fact that we recognize some people as authoritative critics in the "fine" arts but that it would be difficult to reach agreement about who might have similar qualifications in relation to sex.

In the last chapter, I suggest that philosophical theories about sex make an egregious error when they consider it either moral in itself or, as Kant thought, essentially immoral. Kant insists that sex *becomes* moral only in the context of contractual marriage. Together with other difficulties that I touch upon, this causes him to ignore the aesthetic dimensions of sex as well as its capacity to be wholesome and ethically defensible in a plurality of different situations.

As I confess in my concluding remarks, the present book does little more than map out the directions that a more detailed theory of sex would have to investigate at greater length. In the twenty-first century that may be a task some intrepid philosophers will take upon themselves. Those conceptual argonauts deserve our commendation and support. I give them mine well before they venture forth. To the people in my life who have enabled me to write about this perilous subject I offer my enduring gratitude. There is no need to name them in this place.

I. S.

1

Sex, Love, Compassion

Only in recent years have professional philosophers begun to study the nature of sexuality.[1] The analysis of love was a staple of reputable philosophizing from the time of Plato through the age of romanticism and into the twentieth century. Though interest in love as a philosophical topic flagged for several decades, it too is now receiving new attention. Questions about compassion and social feeling related to it have always been treated as legitimate in moral philosophy. But little has been achieved, as yet, in the effort to resolve these fundamental problems about human nature.

In my own writing, which includes efforts in each of these fields, I have sometimes felt that the methodology I pursue, like other philosophers and historians of philosophy, creates an unfortunate hurdle that prevents fullest comprehension. To nonprofessionals as well it has often seemed that, by its very being, philosophy defeats its own aspirations. Phenomena of sex, love, and compassion have such vital impact and pervasiveness for a species like ours that one might well believe that no mode of philosophical analysis can explain them adequately. Such qualms may be justified to some extent. Aside from the limited truth in the Wordsworthian claim that we murder to dissect, all abstract reasoners must recognize that intimate experiences are frequently too elusive or impalpable to be bracketed and inspected with the precision that the valid doing of philosophy requires.

Nevertheless we need not despair. Thinkers as diverse as Plato, Rousseau, Hume, Schopenhauer, and Freud have surely advanced our understanding of sex, love, and compassion. In relation to the work I have done myself, I am (only now) beginning to perceive the cause of my methodological malaise. While trying to make sense of these common aspects of our existence, I have failed thus far to show how they may be *internally* related to each other. In that respect I, like most other philosophers, may indeed have murdered to dissect.

At this stage of the needed investigation, all arguments may have to be sketchy and incomplete. The discussions in this chapter, and in the rest of the book, should be taken as exploratory and often inconclusive. Even so, they can have some utility. If only as a bare grounding, they may prepare us for subsequent work—by others, if not by me— to direct these speculations toward some exhaustive theory that will be meaningful for the twenty-first century.

In examining the inner relations between sex, love, and compassion, it is worth repeating—though it will come as news to no one—that the scientific study of sexuality was one of the outstanding intellectual achievements of the twentieth century. Regardless of the fact that he had predecessors in this field, Freud must always be acclaimed as the great pioneer and principal creator of systematic inquiry about the nature of sex. Before him, the imperious control that sexuality exerts over human feeling and behavior was mainly considered to be a subject matter for poets, novelists, painters, and composers of operas. Imaginative interest in the problematics of sex dates back to the beginnings of their respective art forms. By the eighteenth century artistic freedom reached a point where even lurid sexuality could become an acceptable theme for aesthetic elaboration. In the nineteenth century the attempt to understand the varied characteristics of sex played a role in two divergent movements: the Romantic and the scientific. Both contributed to Freud's intellectual development.

Nineteenth-century romanticism was an offshoot of idealistic philosophy that located the ultimate meaning of life in a metaphysical reality foundational to ordinary experience. In both its optimistic and its pessimistic versions, romanticism interpreted that reality as a kind of love that performed its ontological magic in relations between human beings and in their comprehensive connection to the cosmos. Relying upon Platonic or Christian teaching, the Romantic view of love emphasized the possibility that sexual bonding between men and women might eventuate as a transcendental oneness that would take them beyond merely mundane nature while explaining everything in it. To this extent, romanticism was religious rather than scientific.

At the same time, romanticism was often realistic in its portrayals of the human condition. While being circumscribed by traditional mandates about descriptions of the body and its animality, Romantic literature, painting, even music managed to include honest and often truthful depictions of sexual experience. Romantic realism of this sort sustained and fructified the beginnings of scientific investigation of sex. Though questions about love might still elude the scientific method, the material underpinning of sexuality in our species could be studied like any other mechanism by which the body functions normally.

I do not wish to suggest that sexological science was directly furthered in the nineteenth century by the transcendental component of romanticism. On the contrary, science and the Romantic outlook usually stood in opposition to each other. The struggle to find an accommodation that would eradicate the split between empirical and nonempirical approaches preoccupied many theorists in the nineteenth century. The desired reconciliation became an option only after science had attained social acceptance comparable to the one that religious or quasi-religious doctrines had always had. This achievement occurred in the twentieth century and began more or less with the work of Freud. To date, however, the basic problems in sexual theory have not been solved.

Moving beyond Freud, a hundred years later, we may wonder what would count as an acceptable solution. As long as scientific investigators considered sex a mechanistic syndrome that serves an innate program designed to reproduce the species, the conflict with and within romanticism remained insurmountable. Thinkers like Freud who thought of sex as largely instinctual used that assumption, in conjunction with collateral ideas about human motivation, to attack idealistic concepts that nineteenth-century romanticism had inherited without knowing how to combine them with the methods and the goals of science.

In its most general reference, Freud's paradigm of sex as ultimately reproductive impulse derived from the philosophy of Schopenhauer. Freud says as much in

Beyond the Pleasure Principle, where he defines libido as a manifestation of the primordial and substantially physical life force depicted in Schopenhauer's metaphysics. Though he called this force *Eros*, a term Plato employed to signify organic energy that invests all nature with a search for the highest Good, Freud adhered to Schopenhauer's concept of a purely material will-to-live. In Schopenhauer, and also in Freud, this idea is an article of faith and not scientific. It articulates an unverifiable belief about the whole of reality. As in Plato, it posits that Eros or the will-to-live transcends the world of experience while also causing it to exist. But unlike Plato's thinking, the Schopenhauerian view is radically pessimistic about the cosmic order. Schopenhauer rejected Romantic and religious assurance that the universe is benign or in any way concerned about human values. Freud accepted Schopenhauer's philosophy as an ally in his struggle against religion, which he too condemned as idealistic illusion.

The key to a possible harmonization between science and religion can be found in a particular development of Western thought which arose in romanticism itself. Both the Catholic and the Protestant forms of Christianity had maintained that God is present in the world. This was a difficult notion for orthodox theology to handle. Since the world as we know it is soiled by its materiality, its finitude, its liability to error and to sinfulness, how could it incorporate the divinity in whom a Christian must believe? God was thought to reside in another realm, a reality higher and more sacred than our own. God was perfect in the different types of value that human beings have considered supremely desirable. He was infinitely wise, good, and powerful. He was the absolute manifestation of authentic love.

These divine attributes were thought to validate our confidence that everything that happens in the cosmos, even its recurrent evils and endless tragedies, is for the best in some final manner that we mortals cannot perceive. But if this is so, what sense can it make to say that God himself is *in* the world? If he were, would not his unbounded goodness eradicate the horrors that belong to our vale of tears? And if he tolerates the deficiencies of our daily existence, does that not constitute an imperfection in his being?

Grappling with this problem, Romantic religion of the nineteenth century drew upon ideas of Luther and of Catholic mystics in the Middle Ages, as well as those of philosophers like Spinoza and Hegel. Luther had insisted that human nature, and the world from which it arises, is radically depraved. In their humanity as such, people were incapable of experiencing love. According to Luther, that ability was something only God could have. He is all-loving, indeed love itself, and he remains so eternally and to perfection. He created the world for reasons of love, and he is forever present to it as an expression of his permanent solicitude. When his love infuses a relationship, for instance between man and woman, his presence purifies their union.

In this fashion, Luther held, God's love becomes a human love that the participants, who are only fragile individuals subject to the laws of nature, can attain in no other way. As vessels of the deity's unfathomable bestowal, they embody a value that is flawless and everlasting. It reveals the meaning of life. Even the sexual ingredients of such love are holy because of the sanctity acquired through God's intervention. Employing the Lutheran conception, or a Catholic variation of it, Romantic religion interpreted sexuality as nature seeking the spirituality that emanates from divine love.

By taking this stance, romanticism reinforced idealistic claims that sex is animal impulse in search of love that rises above the merely natural. Though the history of philosophy embroidered that belief with ideas Plato might not have recognized, the view originates with him. Sex was to be reduced to love, not vice versa as materialists like Freud would later assert. But materialists, and naturalists in general, could also agree that beyond its mechanistic apparatus sexuality is able to manifest a striving for a truly meaningful relationship. If, however, we think of love as the satisfaction of this quest, we no longer have to reduce either love to sex or sex to love. The two can be seen as intrinsically interwoven. In that event they avoid, through their effective unity, the conceptual split that could not have been overcome before the advent of romanticism.

In our age, the sectarian religions of the West may still call themselves Christian, but they have been thoroughly modified to accommodate the insights of Romantic revisionism. The mechanistic thesis has also lost its dominance in scientific thinking. Post-Freudians like those who belong to the "object-relations" school study human development not in terms of the libido but rather as a series of explorations toward greater and more consummatory meaningfulness in life.

Following this approach, we find two vistas that open before us and that can lead us on. The first introduces a new definition of sex. It recognizes the importance of libido but emphasizes that libido is not the only kind of sexuality. Libido may continue to be envisaged as a somewhat automatic trigger for generating behavioral and physiological processes related to reproduction.

They in turn create whatever feelings or psychological responses are essential for carrying out this biological mission. Many of the variant patterns in the nature and phenomenology of sex can then be traced to the fact that libidinal energy often goes astray in one or another circumstance and fails to reach the reproductive goal toward which it is innately directed. But having acknowledged this as one of the aspects of sexuality, we can still insist that in the *human* experience of sex other determinants are equally important.

In that vein I elsewhere distinguish the libidinal from what I call the erotic and the romantic.[2] The latter two must also arise, one way or another, from physiological vectors relevant to our sexual being. But these causal ties are not the same as for the libidinal. Even in their fullest activation, the erotic and the romantic may sometimes have little or no significance as far as reproduction of the species is concerned.

The erotic is the affective glue that binds us to other persons, things, or ideals, and to ourselves. It overlaps with social and gregarious feelings that can be enjoyable and are often deeply meaningful in themselves. If I am drawn toward an engaging outline that I see in an abstract painting, I may feel its seductiveness in the marrow of my perceptual being. It is, for me, an erotic object. It has a kind of sexiness or sex appeal that is parallel to the attraction I feel in noticing the shapeliness of a woman's leg. Though my fascination with the leg may have some relation to a libidinal interest of which I am not aware at the moment, that relation can be minimal and even nonexistent. My reaction might only be a response to a lovely design, in this case belonging to a female body, that has appeared in my field of vision and captivated my attention. We need not reduce the erotic quality of this predilection to anything else. To think that the affective power of either a leg or an abstract line in a painting derives from libidinal sexuality is wholly unwarranted. It violates the pluralism that should be our guide.

This applies as well to our experience of the romantic. Through it we are impelled toward persons who matter to us as the particularities we take them to be, whether or not we know what they really are. If our sexual involvement is an obsessive need rather than a means of bestowing value upon the other person, the romantic element can scarcely become an expression of love. Though we may see the individual *as* a person, our attitude belongs to love as well as sex only if we accept him or her as he or she is and not as just an embodiment of appraisive goodness that we desire. But even aside from love, the romantic operates in sexuality alone.

I initially formulated my distinction between the libidinal, the erotic, and the romantic as a means of mapping out different types of love. Having renewed the distinction here in relation to sex as human beings experience it, I now suggest that erotic or romantic sex entails at least a modicum of love, and that this may also be true of the libidinal. But how can this be, one might ask, if—as I just remarked—even the romantic may sometimes occur as a modality in sex taken by itself, and therefore more or less independent of sexual love?

In replying to this challenge, we should begin by noting that nothing in our sexual experience, and virtually nothing that can be called a sex act, exists in total isolation from the rest of life. Human beings are unique in their ability to knit together, in imagination as well as in the qualitative character of each conscious moment, the diverse strands of past events and future possibilities. Awareness might focus upon some arresting object, a woman or a man let us say, that is desired with all the urgency of a libidinal need. But the need, and whatever appears in consciousness as our present drive, is usually affected by erotic and romantic overtones that bespeak our search for love as well as sex.

Even when a sexual impulse is overpowering, it is tinged and generally imbued with a sense of circumambient life that is not limited to sex alone. And since we can hardly separate our immersion in current reality from our longing for ideal completions that may eventuate, our momentary feelings are not only sexual but also inclinations toward some further goal beyond sexuality. The image of this goal is projected from what has happened in our past and may be reconfigured in our future. It is an exemplar of affective possibilities that give meaning to what we feel and what we do. As a part of immediate consciousness, it transforms the raw material of sexuality, whether it be libidinal or erotic or romantic, into an experience that reflects a person's pursuit of love.

Theorists neglect what is distinctively human when they analyze sex apart from this network of ideals and aspirations that control and enrich our sexuality in any situation. People want to be loved, and early on they realize that will not occur unless they reciprocate with a love they have themselves brought into existence. This realization belongs to sexual response as well as to interpersonal reactions that are not sexual. The overly aggressive male or demanding female may not be able to accommodate and personally enjoy the love that resides within human sexuality. But to that extent they are likely to fail, in life as well as in sex.

❊

However greatly love and sex may interweave, we also wish to know whether either of them is significantly related to compassion. It is a very special bond, a type of love but one that is quite different from other types. Compassionate response is often absent in everyday existence. Though reliable statistics are hard to find, we do best to assume from the outset that compassion is not a predominant part of human feeling as a whole.

If we think of sexuality as a taking and receiving of the physical or mental gratification that results from its successful functioning, there would seem to be no justification for expecting sex to be accompanied by a compassionate attitude toward someone else. Compassion means acting on behalf of an individual whose vulnerability and whose place in life we care about. We identify ourselves with that being, though we could easily have ignored the plight of this particular man or woman or other animate creature. In libidinal sex, most obviously, no such feeling may be evident in the disposition of someone who is motivated by a drive to satisfy genital urges. These are programmed to facilitate bodily congress that can lead to reproduction and eventual survival of Homo sapiens. Compassion expresses concern not about our species and its continuation but about a specific living entity, some portion of life that we encounter if only in imagination. Compassion may even thwart the biological ends that libidinal sexuality directly or indirectly points us toward.

But once again, we must consider sex in its overall context, as a pervasive segment of our nature. We are beings who not only wish to partake of consummations that we seek but also to generate them ourselves. In part, at least, we are creators of the enjoyment that our sexuality makes available to us and to others. Our creativity in this regard is itself a consummation, which is not to say that it is just a contrivance for acquiring whatever can be gratifying for ourselves. Though we may get pleasure from giving pleasure, our desire to delight someone else is not entirely reducible to selfish motives of our own. It is a bestowing of value, and therefore constitutes love in at least an incipient form. Even in libidinal sexuality we normally recognize that the object of our desire is someone who matters to us. We may *possibly* see him or her as nothing but a vehicle through which the species perpetuates itself. But that is a remote and very elusive conception. It occurs only sporadically, even in the behavior of a couple who decide to do what is necessary to produce a baby. They are more likely to treat each other as cooperating partners in a process that may culminate in the happy and meaningful family life they want.

This much of sexuality enables compassion to exist as an important factor in it. The sexual object is then taken to be more than reproductive flesh. He or she is experienced not only as a person but also as a joint participant in the biological mysteries of our mutual existence. The physiological dynamics of procreation are oblivious to the pain and even suffering that frequently accompanies them. As if to compensate for this heartlessness of nature, our imagination and our intellect alert us to what the other person undergoes as a fellow prisoner of the sexuality that sweeps through us both. Though it can be great fun, sex is also tension, discomfort, yearning that is not pure pleasure. In its consequences it can be unwanted, sorrowful, even deadly. By warding off these hazards to the other person as well as to ourselves, we enact compassionate feelings that are indigenous to human sexual response, not at all peripheral to it.

Describing this relation between sexuality and compassion, I have concentrated thus far on libidinal sex. The argument becomes even stronger once we consider the erotic and the romantic more thoroughly. That will facilitate our studying the connection between sex, love, and compassion from a somewhat broader point of view.

When libidinal sex overlaps with an expression of compassion, it does so because sexuality in our species can incorporate an attraction toward its recipient *as* a person. This sense of personhood is not always evident at the moment of excitation, and it may sometimes arise as a figment of our imagination. Even so, the human experience of sex is often a mode of attachment to someone who takes on meaning in our lives. To a large degree, the body engorged with sexual desire manifests our normal craving for contact, comfort, and possible oneness with another man or woman. This applies preeminently to the erotic and romantic elements of sexuality. The erotic draws us like a magnet to features of the other person, and not infrequently to that person as a whole. The romantic fixates upon the separate being of the desired individual and awakens our longing for permanent intimacy and affiliation with him or her. The vital flow of intersecting people, each charged with the gravitational force that binds them romantically to each other, makes it possible for sex, or sexual love, or love of any sort, to mean as much as it does to human beings.

Compassion plays an important role in unadorned sex as well as in sexual love because it entails a positive and sustaining attitude toward the creatures we desire and delight in. To appreciate the nature of this response, we must go beyond the analyses I have developed as my previous writing about sex evolved. In my pluralistic fashion, I approached love, sex, and sexual love in a variety of ways: as examples of bestowal and appraisal, as idealizations, as one or another type of imagination, as sensuous or passionate phenomenologies, and as an acceptance (in love of any sort) of what the other is in his or her uniqueness. Compassion lends itself to a comparable gamut of distinctions but also requires something further.

Like all of life, compassion includes an appraisal of what the object of one's attention is worth in relation to oneself. But now this selfish or self-oriented interest becomes secondary to our concern not only to bestow value on the other person, but also to benefit that man or woman through explicit deeds. Having compassion is more than just commending someone for virtues we perceive and helping him or her to overcome defects that he or she may equally lament. In being compassionate, we concentrate on the fact that this person needs to be protected from dangers to which everyone is liable— above all, in moments of desire and intimacy. If we are pessimists like Schopenhauer, we may see life itself as a looming tragedy for all who exist in it. Whether or not we agree with his gloomy vision, however, our compassion implies more than sympathy or some generalized bestowal of value. It also expresses and reveals our readiness to involve ourselves affirmatively through concerted action. Our compassion abides in our willing to perform as circumstances require, and through behavior that manifests our sense of identification, our kindliness, our tenderness, and our friendly intent.

Human sexuality is supremely adept at carrying out this mission. It mobilizes our entire body and mind through gestures that allow us to enjoy the other person while making ourselves available for whatever he or she needs and wants and is capable of directing toward his or her enjoyment. Being what D. H. Lawrence calls "the closest touch of all," it is able to activate and accomplish compassionate stirrings that might have no other outlet.

❋

In mapping the inner relations between sex, love, and compassion, this chapter has dealt only briefly with the nature of sexual love as a whole. I will return to it in later chapters. Here I wanted to emphasize that compassion is a potentiality within sexual experience. Insofar as it too belongs to human sexuality, its kind of love reveals how faulty most philosophies of sex have been. While compassion, sex, and the love that is sexual are not identical, neither are they totally separate from each other. Together with our desire to distinguish clearly and precisely among these motivational systems, we must always remember that in life they interact and interpenetrate dynamically. The feelings or emotions of human beings have their variegated character because of *the different ways* they interact and interpenetrate. With this pluralistic scruple as our touchstone, we can now take some further steps that may also be useful in a theory of sex.

2

Patterns of the Sensuous and the Passionate

The etymology of the terms I use in this chapter is not especially problematic. *Sensuous* derives from the noun *sensation*, meaning a localized experience directly produced through our sense organs. *Passionate* implies powerful emotionality that people undergo on some occasion. But this term, like its noun *passion*, has a subterranean relation to *com*passion which needs some explanation, particularly in view of my comments about the latter in the previous chapter.

Throughout the ancient and much of the modern world, both passion and compassion were officially valued much lower than rationality. As Kant argued at the end of the eighteenth century, only reason could establish the foundations of morality. In traditional philosophy and theology, passion was more often denigrated than compassion. In the West, Judeo-Christianity extolled the man or woman who had compassionate feelings toward other human beings. In the East, Buddhist devotion was primarily directed toward the cultivation of compassion. Partly in the Middle Ages but extensively in the Romantic movements that have waxed and waned for the last two hundred years, passion was idealized beyond compare. In the world that currently exists, sexual passion tends to outweigh compassionate inclinations as a basis for carnal intimacy between spouses or other couples who are closely bonded to each other.

Nowadays people get married, commit adultery, or end their marriages, usually not because they are driven by compassionate sentiments, or anything like them, but rather because they feel the urgency of passion. Before the Romantic revolution in the nineteenth century, the situation was very different. Only in these recent centuries has the human species acquired the belief that a man and woman should become and remain married—or carry out the sexual behavior legitimized by marriage—in adherence to passionate impulse. But since the religion of Romantic passion has been weakened by doubts that were voiced increasingly in the twentieth century, the pendulum of justifiable grounds for human bonding may well swing back again toward compassion—or at least, the feelings of kindliness and friendly compatibility that generally accompany it.

At present I put that question aside. Crucial as it is, the relation between passion and compassion is tangential, not central, to this chapter. In distinguishing here between the sensuous and the passionate, I demarcate attitudes worth considering apart from any connection to compassion that they may also have.

Though they can appear at different times and in different circumstances, the sensuous and the passionate occur in everyone's experience. We encounter one another through our senses, and we enjoy the encounter only as the senses are gratified. We perceive others (and ourselves) through our ability to see, to touch, to hear, to smell, and even to taste. Our sensations are generally localized in specific areas of the body, even though they contribute to responses that unify them into various systems of feeling and awareness.

In sexual behavior, men and women may concentrate upon sensory fulfillment and even seek to prolong it indefinitely. They may give it special importance in their life together, bestow value upon it, create ideals that dignify and further its occurrence. For some people, sexuality amounts to little more than the sensuous, and even the end-pleasure of orgasmic relief becomes subordinate to the delights of intervening sensory enjoyment. For many, however, sex is charged—on occasion, at least—with emotions of yearning, craving, anticipation, hopefulness, or trepidation, and possibly a sense of joyful oneness with another person. In this mode sexuality includes physical and psychological tensions followed by a dying or dissipation of sexual drive through a powerful release of pent-up energy.

This variable complex of warm and turbulent feelings— in contrast to the cooler and less demanding ones that characterize the sensuous—has always been recognized as the passionate aspect of sex. But its relation to instinctual or innate patterns of response has never been understood, nor its dependence upon cultural and environmental influence, nor even its reliance upon the sensuous. In the following chapter I enclose the two modalities within a discussion of sexuality as both interpersonal and appetitive. But first I want to see how they interact.

The passionate requires at least a modicum of the sensuous in order for it to occur. However strong they may be, sexual emotions are always mediated by some type of sensory interest that has been submerged in the needs and consummations of the passionate. For its part, the sensuous would not be felt as sexuality that binds us to another human being unless it also involved the passionate to some degree. Though the two elements may be contrasted, we should not assume that they exist in perfect isolation even when they tend to conflict. Different and separable though these two components often are, they can also cooperate harmoniously within a person's sexuality.

When the sensuous and the passionate are alienated from each other, those who cherish passion may think of the purely sensuous as evil or undesirable. In English the word *sensual* bears that connotation. For their part, those who value the sensuous often feel that the passionate is emotionally aberrant, romantic in a bad sense. But these negative judgments are inaccurate. There is nothing necessarily good or bad in either form of sex. And nothing prevents each from belonging to an attitude of love. That term refers to the *manner* in which we bond with other people, *how* we are sensuous or passionate toward them.

Our most common confusion about sexual love results from the fact that "falling in love" implies a violence of emotional involvement that bespeaks the passionate and may sometimes exclude the sensuous. But falling in love is not the only kind of love, and frequently it is not really love at all. When it entails no clear conception of the other person, it is not love; when it is determined by the lover's need but not the beloved's welfare, it is not love; when it is possessive rather than being a bestowal of value, it is not love. To love another person passionately, one must have both love and passion for that person. But the two are not the same, and passion alone is no guarantee of love.

On the other hand, we often use the word *love* to mean a sensuous interest that one person can have in another. This may or may not be a misuse of the other person; and it may or may not be love in the honorific sense that word usually implies. The sensuous is closely akin to the playful. But one can play with somebody either as a cat plays with a mouse or as a doting mother plays with her baby. Play can be destructive or creative, a hostile confrontation or a wholesome friendliness. When the sensuous effects a mutual enjoyment of, and delighting in, the other person, it instigates a loving attitude no less than the passionate—and whether or not it is accompanied by the passionate.

In the Western world the sensuous and the passionate have often been pitted against each other. Both have been divinized by some people and denigrated by others. For the last two thousand years their partisans have fought in constant warfare. All men and women have participated in the battle; and all have suffered from it. We should not expect to find a single reason for the struggle. At different times, different ideologies have prevailed; and later versions served as reactions to earlier ones. Before describing the psychodynamics of this conflict, I will briefly trace the history of its development without trying to discover a one and only means of explaining it.

If it seems strange to say that love can be sexual and yet not passionate, the reason may reside in ideas we inherited from the past. We have been taught to believe that love as something desirable takes us beyond the pleasures of the senses. The very concept of love as a condition worthy of aspiration arose among people who were ambivalent about the satisfying of bodily desires.

They sought to dignify sex by interpreting it as an ardent need for something else. In the *Phaedrus*, for example, Plato begins with a paradigmatic situation of sexual attraction between two persons. The sensuous components he discounts as merely physical, but the passionate obviously intrigues him. That the lover *yearns* for the beloved signifies to him a search for goodness that underlies all empirical nature. Once the lovers purify their passion by directing it toward the Good itself, their relationship becomes what Plato calls "true love."

Without this transcendental endeavor, Plato thought, passion could only be self-indulgent lust, a burning appetite that can never be fully satisfied. As such, it was something to be feared, avoided, cured, and exorcised like all the other evils of the body. In the ancient world, passion was often seen as insanity. But also it symbolized a "divine madness" that took people out of themselves and enabled them to communicate with the gods. Plato sought to eliminate the materiality of passion by directing it toward an ideal entity—the Good (or Beautiful). That would preserve the value of the passionate, but at the price of making it inhuman and nonsexual. The Good is not a person, and we cannot desire it as we would desire a human being.

In its attempt to rectify the deficiencies of Greek philosophy, Christianity merged Platonism with beliefs taken from the mystery religions of antiquity. These had often celebrated passionate sex both in itself and as the precondition for oneness with a personal deity. Like Platonism, Christianity reviled sexual passion; but like the pagan mysteries, it cultivated the passionate striving for God. In effect, it tried to satisfy sexual longing through the mystical encounter alone.

Though later theologians modified the original design, early Christianity treated man's love for God as a passionate experience that would make all other passionate experiences unnecessary. Not only unnecessary but even harmful to the soul and inevitably sinful. With this restriction the ideal of passion survived though greatly transformed, for now it pertained to love directed toward a spiritual entity. But since that entity was a person, a Supreme Being and yet a person all the same, the ideal could still involve passion not *wholly* different from the passion in sexuality. As Christ had given himself in the nonsexual agony of his Passion, so too would the devout believer achieve salvation through a love that duplicates the union of two passionate lovers and does so at the higher level of pure spirituality.

There were two unfortunate consequences that issued from the Christian idealization of passion. First, it meant that passionate experience as something good was reserved for the love of God to the exclusion of everything and everyone else. Second, it followed that passion directed toward any other object would have to be utterly prohibited. For the ancient world, passion was frightening because it withdrew a man or woman from society and the civilizing company of other people. But for the fledgling Christian devotees its occurrence in sexuality was even worse. It was deemed a sacrilege toward God himself. That is what Saint Jerome meant in his dictum that "he who loves his own wife too ardently is an adulterer." Since our legitimate goal in love can only be oneness with God, passion directed toward another human being—even the person we have married in church—is adultery *more* terrible than enactment of lustful sex with someone who is not our spouse. "A wise man ought to love his wife with judgment, not with passion. Let a man govern his voluptuous impulses, and not rush headlong into intercourse."[1]

This opinion of Saint Jerome was repeated by all the doctors of the church in the Middle Ages. Sexuality itself was not the enemy they fought. They feared, and therefore considered diabolical, the possibility of passionate love between men and women. When Saint Paul said it is better to marry than to burn, he spoke as one who wished to avoid the pleasures as well as the pains of burning. Marriage being a sacrament, the conjugal act could not be sinful in itself. Indeed it was a meritorious way of propagating the species. Nor did most authorities think that sexual impulse was evil. Although there was much debate about whether desire for sexual intercourse preceded the Fall of Adam and whether it was original sin or rather the punishment for original sin, medieval philosophers and theologians generally agreed that sexuality—properly administered—could be innocent.

Saint Thomas insisted that neither the desire for sexual pleasure nor even the pleasure itself was evil, but only the subordination of reason to emotionality that often accompanies them. It was the passionate element of sex that deflected people from their rational search for the Highest Good, thereby leading them into sin or mortal error. As Milan Kundera has recently said about Johannes Scotus Erigena: "What the great theologian found incompatible with Paradise was not sexual intercourse and the attendant pleasure; what he found incompatible with Paradise was excitement."[2]

As a beneficiary of this view, the sensuous could still find a place in Christianity. Sex being a normal part of human nature, sensuous pleasures signified that men and women were doing what they were made to do with the enjoyment that comes from efficiency. The sensuous was not to be pursued for its own sake, but nothing prevented it from fitting into a life directed toward the love of God.

As long as passion did not intrude, bodily delight was morally of little interest to the church; and in fact, sensuous sex was never condemned to the extent that passionate sex was.

As a result, the split between the two modes of sexuality hardened even further; and when the humanization of Christian doctrine occurred in the late Middle Ages, it too divided into separate camps. On the one hand, there were those who tried to elevate sexual love by duplicating within its structure an idea of passion similar to the one that the church reserved for the commendable devotion to divinity. The heresy of courtly love, in the troubadours for example, consisted in the desire to love a woman with the same spiritual yearning that only God deserved. Though the troubadours usually thought of themselves as good Christians, the church considered their humanism an insidious mockery of orthodox belief.

On the other hand, there were those who capitalized upon Christianity's acceptance of the sensuous to make it the principal focus of sexual experience. Alongside of courtly love there arose a benign and breezy attitude toward the nonpassional goodness of sex. Goliardic poetry is filled with it. In the *Carmina Burana* we see its infiltration into the monastery; in Boccaccio and Chaucer it dominates the *Decameron* and *The Canterbury Tales*, though not the *Filostrato* or *Troilus and Criseyde*, which belong to the passionate element. In the *Roman de la Rose*, the first part celebrates the passions of courtly love while the second part (written by another hand) ridicules them for the greater glory of the sensuous.

Within the writings of even the earliest troubadours— Guillaume IX, Marcabru, Cavalcanti, and many others— the two approaches to sexual love occur together, always distinct and different but coexisting as viable alternatives in human relations. Though the troubadours generally favored the passionate over the sensuous, some of their poems make us wonder about their ultimate preference. By the time we reach the Renaissance, it is often impossible, as in the love songs of Lorenzo de' Medici, to determine which of the perspectives is genuine and which is just a poetic façade. Sometimes the two are blended and thoroughly harmonized with each other, in Lorenzo's poetry as well as in the writings of other Renaissance authors.

For the most part, the modern world has retained the division that began in the Middle Ages. Luther and the Reformation as a whole reversed the former tradition in Christianity by insisting that the sensuous is basically as sinful as the passionate. But also, Luther treated sexuality as a natural appetite that becomes dangerous only when its frustration gives it undue importance. It was to be satisfied (twice a week) with a regularity that made emotional extravagance impossible.

At the same time, however, Luther unwittingly enabled the passionate to flourish in a way that it never had before. As we saw in the previous chapter, he argued that although human beings cannot hope to love God, his love descends to the level of humanity and shows itself in the ardent bonds that draw one person to another. This love can manifest itself in society at large, but also between men and women as individuals, particularly in their sexual relations when sanctified by marriage. While people were still deemed sinful in having sensuous desires at all, the passionate union of a married couple could be taken as evidence of their participation in God's love. Possessing this capacity for holiness, passion had only to emancipate itself from the Christian dogmas in order to be idealized on its own.

The liberation of the passionate occurs in the romanticism of the eighteenth and nineteenth centuries. Love then *becomes* God, working miracles through its magical potency. Romantic love defines itself either exclusively as passion or else as the passionate fulfillment of sensuous interests that would be base and even despicable without it. For its part, the sensuous was also liberating itself. In the seventeenth and eighteenth centuries it successfully rebelled against any religious or edifying categories. Though sometimes violent in its rejection of restraints imposed by both the Reformation and the Counter-Reformation, the sensuous cause, as in Montaigne and Rabelais, returned to the medieval belief in the natural goodness of sexual enjoyment. Being nothing but the contact between two epidermises, as Sébastien Chamfort called it, sexuality was thought to have a place within the class of innocent appetites. It was like a taste for mutton or a penchant for lovely colors. If sex inspired powerful emotions, so much the worse. What breaks through the skin can always be painful. Better to limit oneself to pleasures that can be harnessed and easily modified, and in sexuality these are always sensuous.

In subordinating the sensuous to the passionate, or even minimizing the sensuous whenever possible, as advocated by the Romantic puritanism of Rousseau, the nineteenth century wrapped sexuality in an aura of mystery. At one and the same time, it was the holiest and the most forbidding of human activities. Though sexual love purified and ennobled mankind, sex was the one area in which curiosity and personal or even scientific investigation could hardly be tolerated. Novels, dramas, operas, and the ballet concerned themselves with the terrors and the ecstasies of passion, but without being wholly explicit about the sensuous appetitiveness that permeates sex in the real world. We can readily see and hear the passion of Tristan and Isolde, but it is harder to imagine these Wagnerian characters *making* love as other people do. In them, as in many products of latter-day romanticism, passion exists at such an epic distance from the physicality of sex that it mainly appears as a ritual that transcends what is sensuous in actual experience. The passionate once again becomes a part of religion, though now a modern nontheistic religion, instead of being a part of ordinary interpersonal life.

In a young and healthy human being, passion would not depend upon frustration. Between each consummation it would swell as sexual needs are reawakened. But in everyone, passion can be made to flourish as a result of frustration. With its high-minded morality, its Victorian restraints, and its extraordinary sense of decorum, the nineteenth century frequently repressed sensuous expression and thus augmented the passionate. It is almost as if frustration was increased *in order* to create more and greater passion. In any event, that is what happened; and quite clearly it was the passionate element, often but not always spiritualized, that the age valued more than anything else.

The twentieth century has largely been a flight away from passion. Many people nowadays find it all but impossible to take the tragedy of Tristan and Isolde at its face value. We have exploited other, perhaps more pleasant, ways of gratifying our sexual feelings—sensuous ways based upon respect for bodily enjoyment rather than disdain or numinous secrecy that magnifies the emotionality of sex. With its greater tolerance of sexual diversity, the contemporary world may be continuing, and reconstituting, the attitude of the swinging eighteenth century. But the experience of romanticism has not been forgotten, and in the present-day acceptance of the sensuous we may be closer to a wholesome reconciliation than at any time in the past.

Without the sensuous, sexual experience would not have the kind of goodness that it often has for human beings. It would be a venting of propellant force, a gnawing hunger, a savage drive that comes upon people for reasons too deep to fathom—an instinctive and variably intense compulsion issuing from organic springs that may scarcely enter into consciousness. Without the passionate, sexual involvement might be agreeable enough but not especially urgent or meaningful. It would be calm, relaxing, delectable, and quieting to the nerves though also affording moments of exquisite, even excruciating, sensory pleasure. The sensuous aspect of human sexuality must surely resemble what monkeys and apes experience while being groomed by each other.

To Western man the sensuous has frequently seemed passive, unworthy of a questing spirit. Like Odysseus in the land of the lotus-eaters, we feel threatened by the tranquilizing effect of mere sensuousness, and by the fact that getting something directly through the senses is rarely as challenging as yearning for it in erotic imagination. This applies to the ancients as well as the moderns. No one is surprised to hear Byron say that "passion is the element in which we live: without it we but vegetate";[3] but even Plutarch approvingly reports that Lycurgus recommended continence in newly wedded Spartans because "it continued in both parties a still burning love and a new desire of the one to the other."[4]

Neither Lycurgus nor Plutarch believed that passion is "the element in which we live," that it defines the normal or appointed function of sexuality. Yet they realized that intimacy seems more valuable to husband and wife when they desire each other ardently. The passionate always runs the risk of being painful or mad; but it yields a sense of importance that cannot come from the sensuous alone. All the same, the sensuous provides immediate gratification as well as incandescent beauty. Though it may seem mindless and superficial, it satisfies a network of needs and appetites no less than food or drink.

In sexual experience, the sensuous functions in two ways. First, it is extremely effective in eliciting libidinal attraction. It arouses the male or female, intensifies their awareness of each other, and brings the genitals into a stimulated condition that is requisite for their satisfactory operation. In men the visual and auditory senses are highly developed as an agency of sensuousness. The erotic scopophilia, love of looking, that characterizes the human male serves as an anticipatory response to sexual possibilities. Whether he is sitting at a café, waiting for a train, walking through a shop, looking at a painting, or watching a movie, the male uses his eyes for visual consummations that are inherently sexual even if they do not lead to orgasm.

Compared to men, or themselves in nonsexual situations, women are less obviously aroused by sensations of sight or hearing. They tend to rely more on physical contact. In both men and women, but especially in women, the tactile sense facilitates like nothing else that "closest touch" to which I referred. Directly or indirectly, proximately or at a distance, these sensuous acuities create the phenomenological parameters of sexual experience. And within the experience itself, foreplay augments desire by means of the sensuous. Looking, touching, tasting, hearing, smelling—each in accordance with individual preference and momentary feeling—brings about a heightening of interest in the other person and in his or her sexual availability. Without sensuous foreplay, coitus might occur in ways that could propagate the species. But unless there were some prelude of this sort, however brief or limited, sexual intercourse would be less enticing for either male or female.

The existence of this hedonic possibility indicates the second function of the sensuous. Quite apart from its capacity to awaken libidinal appetite, the sensuous can be joyful in itself. The man who watches a woman undress may do so for the sake of stimulating himself; but more often, he savors the somewhat passive goodness of looking. The naked body, when it is handsome or suggestive, is an agreeable thing to see. Observing it need not lead on to anything else. It would be a pity to live with nothing but the sexual delight of looking, peering, watching. But one does not have to justify such responses by citing another end to which they lead. Their value consists in their enjoyability as mainly sensuous moments for men and women, and not as mere instrumentalities.

In coitus itself, the sensuous does more than just elicit a genital drive. It also has its own ability to gratify sexual inclinations. The tensions that sensuous foreplay evokes can lead to an orgasmic release that results from excitation of the sense organs rather than a passionate longing or any vehement pursuit of explosive end-pleasure. Even when the orgasm is felt as a culmination that convulses one's entire being, its effects are partly localized in erotogenic sensations and these are not always accompanied by strong emotions. In the passionate mode, orgasms can be overwhelming. Nevertheless, they may not be more satisfying, and often they are less enjoyable, than the pleasures of the sensuous. Some people relinquish passionate possibilities for the sake of having sensuous consummations that are easier to attain or more desirable under the circumstances.

For many persons, however, sexual behavior would not be satisfying unless it also involved the kind of emotional discharge that the passionate offers. The sensuous then functions not only to create desire and to proffer hedonic goods that come from its occurrence, but also to guide libidinal cravings toward a final release that takes them beyond sensation. Without the mediation of the senses, we would not exist for one another. But our affinity as human beings is more than just sensory. People gravitate within each other's sexual orbit through an urgency and importance that cannot be fully explained in terms of sight or touch or any other sense.

This mutual longing is a need for consummatory completion of tensions that are simultaneously both appetitive and interpersonal. Yearning becomes stronger as the tensions increase; if they are not released properly, sexual impulse will not infrequently turn into anger and hatred. And since frustration or orgasmic failure are always possible, the striving for fulfillment may be accompanied by fear long before any resolution is even feasible. In the male, this can result in impotence; in the female, in a thwarting of desire that makes it difficult for some women to be sexually excited.

In either event, passion disappears and the sensuous is undermined as well. But often these two are mutually supportive. The sensuous induces sensory alertness, which may then be experienced as passionate need; the passionate thrusts the sexes into each other, and this may occasion sensuous gratification as well as emotional ecstasy. Insofar as the sensuous and the passionate define different modalities, they are separable. To some degree, each can survive without the other. How they may be harmonized, and whether they should be, is one of the major problems for philosophy as well as sexology.

Since the two types of sexuality interweave so massively, we may wonder why they do separate and conflict. Left to itself, would not sexual experience bring about their harmony and joint cooperation? But sexuality cannot be left to itself; it does not exist apart from the rest of human nature. We men and women differ from all other animals, including the nonhuman primates, inasmuch as our sexual responsiveness pervades each moment and every aspect of our being. In saying this, I am agreeing with the "pansexual" view of human nature—the idea that sex permeates our entire life in one fashion or another. I will return to that conception later in this book. We must also recognize, however, that throughout our daily life sex frequently vies with other interests. It is a threat to many economic, political, social, and spiritual aspirations whose goals are not consistent with either the sensuous or the passionate.

Civilization in general has evolved as a panoply of institutions that often restrain the sexual in order to accentuate something else. This does not mean that civilization must be repressive. It can further each mode of sexuality, and in some respects it always has. Furthermore, the conflict between sensuous and passionate may not be wholly caused by societal repressiveness. Even if some utopia were to dedicate itself to the harmonization of them, and to the greatest expression of each, there may be something in sexuality itself that can always renew their internal warfare. I want to consider what that might be, and whether it is related to what Freud called "organic repression."

❅

If it were easy to harmonize the sensuous and the passionate, many of the problems of sexuality would disappear. But the fact that mighty ideologies have been constructed out of the desire to part them, and to favor one rather than the other, suggests that something very profound impedes an adequate harmonization. In his usual pessimism about sexual happiness, Freud often stressed the difficulties in satisfying the two modes of sexuality. Discussing the relationship between freedom and total satisfaction, he remarks that not only repression is injurious to human beings but also unfettered sexual liberty. He then says:

> The value the mind sets on erotic needs instantly sinks as soon as satisfaction becomes readily obtainable. Some obstacle is necessary to swell the tide of the libido to its height; and at all periods of history, wherever natural barriers in the way of satisfaction have not sufficed, mankind has erected conventional ones in order to be able to enjoy love. This is true both of individuals and of nations. In times during which no obstacles to sexual satisfaction existed, such as, may be, during the decline of the civilizations of antiquity, love became worthless, life became empty, and strong reaction-formations were necessary before the indispensable emotional value of love could be recovered. In this context it may be stated that the ascetic tendency of Christianity had the effect of raising the psychical value of love in a way that the heathen antiquity could never achieve; it developed greatest significance in the lives of the ascetic monks, which were almost entirely occupied with struggles against libidinous temptation.[5]

The obstacles to which Freud refers are the repressive controls that are able to increase passion. In claiming that they are needed for the "indispensable emotional value of love" and "to swell the tide of the libido to its height," he would *seem* to be arguing for the desirability of the passionate as well as the sensuous. But even so, Freud's statement implies that they cannot both be satisfied. If sexual satisfaction is readily obtainable, the sensuous can be fully gratified; but then, Freud assures us, passion disappears and sex ceases to be valuable. Without the barriers of frustration and restraint, love becomes "worthless." For it to recover its emotional importance, sexuality has to defeat its own ends, as in the extreme case of Christian asceticism. When that happens, however, the pleasures of the sensuous are also denied. By choosing lesser obstacles to satisfaction, Freud might have envisaged a condition in which some passion, at least, would be compatible with sensuous enjoyment. But in this place, he sounds as if the mere fact of being available without obstacles deprives sexual experience of its value in either mode.

Freud's argument is plausible from the point of view of those who identify love with passion and think that passion can only originate through obstacles. If this were true, love would lose its value once the obstacles that create passion have been removed. Like many another raised in the nineteenth century, Freud states more than once that a woman can expect to lose her lover on the very day that she takes him as her husband. He obviously means a lover not in the sense of one who *loves* the woman, but rather in the sense of passionate sexual ardor.

To those who believe in the sensuous, it will seem strange that sexual love should thus be tied to passion alone. Through the intimacy that marriage affords, lovers can have access to more sensuous opportunities than could ever have existed at a distance. Having surmounted the obstacles that kept them apart, they may enjoy the pleasures of the senses with greater reliability, greater leisure, and greater likelihood of success. Provided, of course, that sensuousness is valued in itself. If so, the love that it defines can never be worthless to those who pursue the sensuous with utter freedom.

But while Freud neglects the goodness of purely sensuous love, he is not an advocate of passion either. From the paragraph I just quoted, one might have thought he would be. Reared in the Romantic tradition, he turns against it as one of its most profound critics. In many places he seems horrified at the anguish and emotional stress that passion brings to life. Though sexuality sinks in value once obstacles are removed, Freud is sensitive to how greatly the obstacles cause misery and neurosis. In this, he closely resembles Lucretius, who also thought that the power and significance of passion derive from the frustration of sexual impulses. Lucretius extolled the sexual regularity in marriage, but only because it *eliminates* passion. In the opinion of both Freud and Lucretius, romantic love is not really valuable but only valued, or overvalued, by the passionate interest. This has the effect of swelling the tide of the libido. Since that has so many uncontrollable consequences, however, neither Lucretius nor Freud believes it can result in sexual happiness.

At other times, Freud seemed to hold views of a totally different kind. Together with his pessimism, and even negativism, one also finds indications that he may have surmised that harmony between the sensuous and the passionate is sometimes possible. When he lists the ingredients in a happy marriage, or what he calls the "completely normal attitude" toward sex, he mentions a fusion of *Sinnlichkeit* and *Zärtlichkeit*.[6] The latter is tenderness or affection. His translators render the former as *sensuality*; but since Freud uses the word with no pejorative intention, I think my term *sensuousness* is more appropriate. The question now arises: Does the fusion of Sinnlichkeit and Zärtlichkeit also include the passionate? Freud was not writing with my distinction in mind, and one cannot hope to answer such a question too precisely. But in describing what he considers to be normal sexuality, Freud cites obstacles to final satisfaction that would necessarily foster the passionate throughout maturity. Tracing adult libido to infantile demands that are unrealistic as well as unsatisfiable, he remarks that sexuality as a whole is therefore inherently imperfect, inherently incapable of being fully satisfied.

Whether this condition follows from organic repression Freud does not say, but he does refer to universal incest-taboos as the basis of childhood yearnings that forever linger on in the libido of adults. If this is true, the structure of all sexual drive would seem to generate passion from within itself. If the sought-for individual is always and essentially an image of a parental figure, as Freud insists, sensuous desire *must* be accompanied by some amount of passionate yearning for an unobtainable person. That in turn can prevent even sexual experience that is readily available from losing value or becoming worthless.

Given Freud's belief in parental images and their effect upon the emotions, it is likely that he did mean to include the passionate as well as the sensuous in the sexuality of a happy marriage. Discussing the merging of Sinnlichkeit and Zärtlichkeit, he remarks that the libidinal personages of maturity "will still be chosen on the model (imago) of the infantile ones, but in the course of time they will attract to themselves the affection that was tied to the earlier ones. A man shall leave his father and his mother—according to the biblical command—and shall cleave unto his wife; affection and sensuality are then united. The greatest intensity of sensual passion [*"sinnlicher Verliebtheit"*] will bring with it the highest psychical valuation of the object—this being the normal overvaluation of the sexual object on the part of a man."[7]

In speaking of "overvaluation," Freud confuses us again. He uses that term throughout his writings to signify an unwarranted expenditure of libido. It is the dangerous and unrealistic component in romantic attachment; it is the madness in what is known as "falling in love." When Freud condemns passion, he does so because he thinks it always leads to overvaluation.[8]

Nevertheless, what Freud says in this place would definitely imply that normal sexuality satisfies both the sensuous and the passionate by choosing as its recipient a person who reawakens childhood cravings while also being quite accessible. And perhaps it is this theme that we ought to emphasize in his speculations. Far from forcing us to assume that the sensuous and the passionate are necessarily antagonistic, his argument would encourage us to find the conditions needed for them to cooperate. Despite his ambiguities, I believe that was Freud's intention. But he did not carry it to completion, and our age will have to find its own ways of making that attempt.

❄

It is still too early in the development of the life sciences for us to resolve the difficulties we have been examining. But I would like to walk about them a little longer, in the hope of understanding them better.

I begin, or begin again, by asserting that prima facie the sensuous is not intrinsically vicious. It is just a playful enjoyment of the body, and of the human personality as it expresses itself through the senses. The sensuous is an aesthetic phenomenon whose materials are sensations related to either the genitals or other erotogenic zones. Whether its pleasures are orgasmic or not, whether it limits itself to foreplay or goes beyond, whether it is experienced with a single partner or many at once, whether it is heterosexual or homosexual, whether it employs the mouth, the anus, the vagina, or any other orifice of the body, it can be characterized as a versatile acuity capable of maximizing and prolonging human consummations.

When Ovid speaks of the "art of love," he principally has in mind this aspect of sexuality. And as savages have often been idealized as living at the level of mere sensation, the sensuous is frequently represented by an idyllic image of primitives in nature. Thus Stendhal, who distinguishes between sensuous love, passionate love, vanity love, and sympathy love, depicts *l'amour sensuel* as an erotic extension of the hunt: "Whilst out shooting, to meet a fresh, pretty country girl who darts away into a wood. Everyone knows the love founded on pleasures of this kind: however unromantic and wretched one's character, it is there that one starts at the age of sixteen."[9] In the visual arts, we often encounter a similar scene. Watteau, Boucher, and Fragonard captured it to perfection.

Stendhal himself wishes to transcend the sensuous in the direction of the passionate. But nowhere does he insist upon a necessary conflict between the two. And though his entire book on love is devoted to the possibilities of passion love, he also knows that it can sometimes be harmful in thwarting a person's sensuous nature. In the chapter entitled "Failures" in *De l'Amour*, he shows how too much passion can cause male impotence resulting from a fear of performance, thereby robbing the lovers of sensory enjoyment. And despite his faith in passion as such, Stendhal continually makes statements like this one: "Some virtuous and affectionate women have almost no idea at all of sensuous pleasure; they have only very rarely laid themselves open to it, if I may put it so, and even then the raptures of passion love have almost made them forget the pleasures of the body."[10] When he discusses the birth of love, Stendhal gives the sensuous at least as much importance as the passionate: "To love is to derive pleasure from seeing, touching, and feeling through all one's senses and as closely as possible, a lovable person who loves us."[11]

Stendhal does not take the defense of the sensuous any further. In his novels, its nature and its consequences are always tantalizingly unclear. But in seeking to harmonize it with passion love, he accords the sensuous a dignity that many of his contemporaries found shocking. In Eastern philosophy this dignity has often turned into spiritual idealization, the sensuous being refined into a method for *extirpating* passionate cravings. In the sexual yoga of Hinduism, Buddhism, and Taoism, male and female bodies achieve spiritual oneness through a spontaneous and unforced sharing of their interest in the senses. Intercourse occurs not through any action or doing, not because of any "grasping desire," but rather as a passionless experience of sensuous love: "One finds out what it can mean simply to look at the other person, to touch hands, or to listen to the voice. If these contacts are not regarded as leading to something else, but rather allowed to come to one's consciousness as if the source of activity lay in them and not in the will, they become sensations of immense subtlety and richness."[12]

In depicting the sensuous as they do, the Eastern philosophers have one thing in common with Western hedonists like Ovid. As in much erotic literature both Eastern and Western, they strengthen the sensuous element by making sexual behavior routine and even casual—though also very sophisticated in the augmenting of pleasure. But easygoing sex is rarely cathartic; and cleverness in the use of the body need not result in powerful emotions. Can anyone following minute instructions about positions and techniques, of the sort that are found in the *Kama Sutra* for instance, really get carried away by an intense longing for the beloved? Delightful and even exquisite lovemaking can be taught, but not passion. The same applies to most contemporary sex manuals. Readers of them may learn a great deal that can liberate their propensity to sensuous gratification. But though these books may succeed in making sexuality less troublesome, less inhibited, and less frightening, they can do little to facilitate passionate response.

Perhaps for this reason, therapeutic advice that has emanated from experimental research in the last few decades often appears to question the desirability of passion. In their book on sexual inadequacy, Masters and Johnson caution against the "pattern of demanding pelvic thrusting" in which libidinal passion generally manifests itself: "The wife repeatedly must be assured that this forceful approach will not contribute to facility of response. If the husband initiates the driving, thrusting coital pattern, the wife must devote conscious effort to accommodate to the rhythm of his thrusting, and her opportunity for quiet sensate pleasure in coital connection is lost."[13] This concern about "sensate focus," and sensuousness in general, can be interpreted as primarily therapeutic; but there may be no way of differentiating between therapeutic means and permanent conditioning in the responsiveness of those who adhere to that advice.

Since passion can originate in pathology, we may not want to increase it on all occasions. When it does occur, however, it involves something that goes beyond knowledge of sensuous techniques. It entails a *longing* for the person one is with, a *striving* for the deepest contact, and in heterosexual situations a *yearning* to penetrate her and to be penetrated by him. Through passion people enact a need for emotional union that enables each to participate in the other, to appropriate the other and possibly to give oneself as well.

Whence arises this passionate attraction that human beings have toward each other, and that they express in sexuality? From person to person the phenomenon varies widely. Some theorists postulate a fixed quantity of passional drive with which an individual is endowed. If this were the case, passion would be an emotional constant for each individual, analogous to innate temperament or musical talent or mathematical aptitude. As there are volatile spirits and others that are more sedate, so too would people be by nature either more or less passionate. At the same time, however, we know that sexual passion is correlated with physiological maturation. In men and women who are repressed in the manner that characterizes modern civilization, passion extends from adolescence into middle age. The time span differs vastly, but most young adults go through a period of passionate potential that eventually becomes kinetic in relation to at least one erotic object.

Through the middle years passion tends to diminish, though the onset of menopause makes the decline more noticeable in women than in men. In both sexes the trend can often reverse itself in the thirties, the forties, or even later, with an outburst of sexual fervor that some writers call the middle-age adolescence. As if to compensate for the gradual loss of emotional capability, nature gives men and women another chance to feel toward some beloved the youthful turmoil that fascinates everyone but no one manages perfectly when it first occurs.

Fictional literature frequently centers about the vicissitudes of human sexuality at these two periods in a person's life. They set the biological time for tragedy as well as comedy. We would have difficulty understanding *Phaedra* in any of its versions unless we realized that the heroine has reached the time of sudden recrudescence in passion that many women experience as they approach the menopause. On the other hand, the dilemma that Shaw's doctor undergoes in *The Doctor's Dilemma* might not have existed if Ridgeon were either younger or somewhat older. Having reached the age of forty in a celibate condition, Ridgeon complains of a curious and unlocalized "aching." Sir Patrick, his venerable colleague, correctly diagnoses the ailment: "It's very common between the ages of seventeen and twenty-two. It sometimes comes on again at forty or thereabouts. You're a bachelor, you see. It's not serious—if you're careful."[14]

Though geared to physiological developments common to the species, these temporal factors are also a function of social and psychological determinants. Some people never fall in love, others seem to do so all the time. Furthermore, passionate desire is so highly prized by men and women in the Western world that a great deal of effort goes into trying to reinstate it throughout the years of maturity. What came so effortlessly in early youth has to be carefully nurtured later on. The details of this nurturing process are analyzed magnificently in Proust's account of Swann's love for Odette. Even in first love, however, passion is psychogenic to a considerable degree.

The psychiatrist Theodor Reik argued that passionate love arises as part of an adolescent's attempt to satisfy some ego ideal. Having been defeated in our childhood quest for self-perfection, he says, we transfer the embodiment of the ego ideal to another person. Since nobody can provide the perfection that we seek, love must always be illusory: "All love is founded on a dissatisfaction with oneself. It is an attempt to escape from oneself in search of a better, an ideal self. The lover imagines that he has found it in his object. Is love thus an illusion? Of course it is."[15] Romantic love, which Reik identifies with falling in love, would thus differ from other love only in its emotional ferocity. Its enormous power Reik explains as an effort, a desperate effort, to rescue one's menaced ego by striving to appropriate the perfect goodness promised by some illusory image of another person.

But even at its most ardent, love need not be considered an illusion. Morever, "falling in love" is not the same as "*being* in love" and "*staying* in love."[16] And Reik is also mistaken when he claims that without personal dissatisfaction there would be no passion. Strong sexual feeling is part of the sheer vitality that almost *everyone* prizes, not just those who are debilitated psychologically. Passional impulse is not greater in people who are dissatisfied with themselves, or diminished in those who are not dissatisfied. It is true that passion implies an ardent need. Unless one wants the woman or man, this particular woman or man at this particular moment, one will not have a passionate desire. But we need not assume there is a perfection that we lack, that causes us to be dissatisfied with ourselves, and that we hope to attain by possessing the other person.

In feeling passion, we seek a unity with some man or woman. That is what we wish to experience as the goal of our emotion. For that reason, making love is more than just the removing of a dissatisfaction. It can also be the creating of an emergent good, an affective bond, valuable in itself whether or not it is the remedy for a menaced ego. The ego may be menaced if it has no passionate inclinations. But except in pathological cases, passion does not itself exist as merely a device for escaping prior failures in oneself.

Passion causes us to *care* about people, to care about their needs and their desires, to want them and to want to be wanted by them. It overcomes loneliness and isolation by making us eager to be with other men and women. It provides the impetus without which we could not identify with fellow creatures struggling like ourselves in a world we did not make or ever choose. At this point passionate sex is enriched by our sense of compassion, with all that it implies about the possibility of friendliness and loving-kindness. If we had no such feelings, could people even be persons who matter to us? Could we be persons for them? Would an authentic love of persons be possible?

The answers to these questions may be affirmative insofar as the sensuous mode can instill its own sociable joys and mutually compassionate consummations. These are often gentler and more subdued than those that issue from the passionate. But without the animal warmth of passion, would the sensuous be able to mold and solidify the interhuman bonding that ordinarily belongs to the very concept of a person?

Since the beginning of time, human beings have always searched for ways to increase passionate desire in themselves and in someone else. One could write a history of our species by reference to love potions alone. Even those who idealize the sensuous recognize the importance that passion has for most people. In his book

The Physiology of Marriage, Balzac defines love as the poetry of the senses; yet he frequently reminds us that even sensory pleasure deteriorates unless passion is also present. In the Western world men have customarily sought to ignite the female's adoration of them by flaunting their social status among other men, whereas women were expected to intensify male sexuality through the allure of their feminine face and figure.

Liberated women who nowadays complain that men have treated them like things to be used are right to protest against the indignities to which they have been subjected. But they will never understand this situation unless they realize that these roles have existed because women had no other way of procuring male attachment or making themselves desirable to members of either gender. In what served for centuries as the rudimentary sex act, the female did not need to do anything, while the man had to have an erection. This was more likely to occur if he felt secure and even admirable in being masterful. For reasons of their own, sometimes good and sometimes bad, women (not all women, but many) have been willing to submit to almost anything that will bring about that feeling in the male, and so augment his ardor for themselves as females.

As an example of this sociobiological phenomenon, we need only consider the institution of the dancing-girl or striptease artist. With their voracious sexual appetite for visual sensations, men enjoy the exhibition of female flesh, and in most societies more than women enjoy seeing male flesh. In all societies, women have regularly provided such entertainment. At the same time, the self-exhibiting female systematically hides as much as she reveals. She causes frustration through her teasing and ambiguously inviting gestures, through the repressive suggestion that there is something naughty or forbidden in the showing of her nudity, and through the distance that her performance imposes upon an audience that can watch but cannot touch her. Evasiveness of this type may perturb a man but it does not threaten him. The performance is itself a means of flattering his sexual dominance. It arouses desire, and sometimes passion, that he usually welcomes.

Dancing-girls and stripteasers make up a tiny percentage of the female population. Moreover, they are relegated to the lower classes as a way of assuring men that the male is ultimately superior to the female despite her great attractiveness. But the dancing-girl is symbolic of many other women insofar as she specializes in catering to masculine interests through the willing presentation of her body. That is one of the principal functions that society has relegated to women in general. The equivalent among men—crooners, movie idols, and others who devote themselves to the evocation of sexual desire in women—have no comparable importance. They do not represent attitudes that have been expected of all men or even most.

On the contrary, men who excite women just by titillating them have generally been scorned by other men, and sometimes hounded by society as in the Don Juan myth. Men have wanted women to be passionate, but only when they adulate achievements that belong to the world of men and that men themselves can admire. The male who is a professional lover does not live in that world, at least not in the way that the politician, the soldier, and the basketball player do.

In large part, this differential is culturally constructed. At the same time, however, it was (and still is) related to the fact that women had reason to fear the consequences of their passion. Particularly in the past, they yielded to its ecstatic abandon only when they could feel protected by a vigorous and socially successful male. Don Juan seduces them by pretending to be that kind of man. Eventually his victims learn that he is not, and that he has only been simulating sexual passion toward them. The women finally see that he is passionate only about the fleeting joys of sensuous dalliance that he himself experiences. Not surprisingly, they turn on him with all the fury that unrequited passion has created in them.

❊

As Freud suggests in the passage I quoted earlier, natural barriers and artificial obstacles can increase passion and magnify its value. In the Western world the tradition that stems from Plato sets up obstacles by means of the very idealizations that structure its attitude toward love. Plato defines eros as the desire for the Good; but then he tells us that the Good is unattainable in experience. All human desire must therefore be a searching for perfection that is both hopeless and inescapable. If one could really live this philosophy, one's life would be a throbbing passion from beginning to end. That being impossible, courtly and Romantic attitudes toward love make lesser arrangements among mere human beings. Like Platonism, they cultivate the passionate by means of alternate inducements and repressions not wholly different from the striptease. The medieval lady was revered by the troubadours as the visible exemplar of beauty but always worshipped from afar, suitable for poetic imagination but never to be touched or enjoyed through sexual intercourse.

In other versions of courtly love, the beloved was more accessible. Nevertheless she was often fitted into a pattern of idealization that was inherently Neoplatonic and/or Christian. In the nineteenth century, the various courtly concepts were democratized so that every woman could become an angel in the household. She was to shine forth as the image of a perfect goodness men desired, especially if she herself was not prone to sexuality that might have quieted her husband's endless yearnings. Her repressed condition and theoretical lack of carnal appetite served as a limiting obstacle that men frequently employed to maximize their own passion. When the authentic feelings, sensuous or passionate, of a healthy woman burst through the conventional barriers, she was made to feel guilty or sick. Not until the twentieth century did Western society admit that the lustful woman is far from being abnormal, anymore than the lustful man.[17]

In our day the women's liberation movement, and above all the greater strength and security of the female, may provide (may, in part, even be designed to provide) a new enticement to the male. The equalization demanded by contemporary women can therefore be a change of tactics that increase the likelihood of sexual fulfillment. Whatever their individual orientation may be, women in various countries are freer now than ever before to gratify their sexuality as they wish. And so are men. The older barriers no longer exist as once they did. We shall all have to seek new means of attaining sex that is vibrant and meaningful as well as delectable.

With this in mind, we can begin by recognizing that Plato might well have been right to associate passion with a search for ideals. Though the notion of the Good is too amorphous to be of much use, it may be true that without standards of value there would be no passion in human beings. The passionate in sex is not wholly reducible to a drive for coitus, or an instinct for orgasmic consummation. These may serve as regular concomitants of libidinal passion, but they themselves presuppose a wanting to unite and a belief in the importance of that goal. Passion does not arise unless the object of desire, or the activity of uniting, or both, are considered *worthy* of being desired.

This basic valuation can occur in any number of biological, psychological, and sociological manifestations. But they are not always the same, and no one of them is either necessary or sufficient. There must be something in valuation *itself* that engenders the passionate. In a healthy organism passion occurs spontaneously during the years of sexual maturity, and not entirely because of artificial barriers. If this statement is correct, perhaps its truthfulness results from the fact that healthy organisms create standards of value as part of their innate response to reality. Far from being artificial, the social restraints that foster passion may themselves devolve from a programmed need in men and women alike to make ideals of one sort or another.

This suggestion is only speculative, however, and will remain so until it can be verified by the empirical sciences. The most intriguing problems about human sexuality are both sexological and philosophical. They are all related to the conflict between the sensuous and the passionate; but they also involve confusions in our assumptions about libidinal drive, erotic attraction, romantic oneness, sexual goodness, and above all the nature of sex itself.

In the male and in the female, the sensuous and the passionate operate through different behavioral dispositions and different orgasmic and nonorgasmic responses that need to be delineated with as much precision as theorists can presently achieve. If the passionate is "natural" in the sense of being more than just a product of artificial barriers, we must determine what its natural condition may be. Moreover, as we shall see in a later chapter, the usual distinction between the natural and the unnatural will itself have to be reexamined.

Since the sensuous and the passionate conflict in so much of human experience, we must try to discover how they can be harmonized. But it is also possible that harmonization is not desirable, or even feasible, for all people on all occasions. In formulating a pluralistic approach to sex, we cannot presuppose that any one solution is necessarily best for every situation. Human nature is too diversified for us to believe anything like that.

3

The Nature and Evaluation of Sex

When Schopenhauer analyzed the nature of love, in his chapter "The Metaphysics of Love Between the Sexes," he claimed to be the first philosopher to have revealed the secrets of sexual love.[1] Outrageous as his boast may have been, it was accurate in one respect: no philosopher before Schopenhauer had reduced, as thoroughly as he, romantic, marital, or interpersonal love to an underlying and metaphysically ultimate force of libidinal sexuality. This idea, which people in the twentieth century have often ascribed to Freud, was recognized by Freud himself as a conception he acquired from Schopenhauer.

Having criticized in other books the reductivism of both Schopenhauer and Freud, I have no need to do so here. Instead I wish to propose a general view of sex that cuts across the differences between their ideas and mine. If I succeed in this, my formulation can possibly buttress many of our joint analyses. There are at least two kinds of questions that must be asked. First, what is the nature of sex, particularly in human beings; and second, how can we determine which among our variegated sexual acts and experiences are *inherently* better or worse than others?

These questions, and the subsidiary queries they induce, are not entirely independent of each other. They all differ from questions we may also ask about moral, social, or religious standards superimposed upon sexuality as regulative principles that usually assert some derivation from a higher goodness. Such principles are "idealizations," in my usage of that term. They are the means by which human beings create and then pursue elevated goals that make life meaningful for themselves and other people. Though the relevant standards are not necessarily falsifications of anything, neither are they mandates etched in objective reality. However greatly they may alter sex as it exists in our species, they are nevertheless external to its being.[2]

To know what there is about sex that can make it better or worse apart from such external considerations, we need to clarify our thinking about the indigenous character of this range of feeling and behavior. At least at a prima facie level, the evaluation of sex must issue out of our views about the nature of sexuality in itself. This is largely a problem for ontology. It is fraught with the perils and the limitations of that branch of philosophy.

Throughout my discussion, I assume that the reader will intuitively appreciate the differences between issues that are evaluative and those that are not. Since I believe they are inevitably interrelated, I will be analyzing coordinates that pertain equally to both. As philosophers or just reflective men and women, we may often wonder whether any one occasion of sex is intrinsically better than some alternative. From the point of view of sexuality alone, should we or should we not believe that all the phenomena that people call sexual—among which we would have to include autoeroticism, fetishism, bestiality, and sadomasochism—are equally good as *sex*? Or are some more desirable in themselves? And within the class of statistically normal behavior, is one or another type inherently preferable? Is any object of sexual interest uniquely worthy of being chosen?

In undertaking this inquiry, we put aside for the moment the questions about social, ethical, and religious implications of sex to which I referred. Important as they are and worthy of being studied in their own context, those questions are extraneous to the present speculation. They are not directly pertinent to the study of human sexuality as a common faculty that yields within itself a basis for assessing the independent goodness or badness of different sex acts.

Heterosexual coitus, for instance, may be morally desirable under some circumstances but not under others. Premarital sex may be encouraged or condemned because of its effect upon institutions like traditional matrimony. Homosexuality may be recommended or attacked because of its tendency to separate the sexes. A society that is trying to lower its level of population might favor homosexuality while another that wants to increase the number of child births might reward every kind of heterosexual behavior, including extramarital lovemaking. Let us say that we agree about these matters. Even so, questions about intrinsic value would still remain. Sex does not exist in total isolation from the rest of life, and yet its goodness must arise from something in its structure that distinguishes it from everything else. How then shall we discover which sexual activities are valuable in themselves? How can we know that any are better than others? Addressing these issues will help us delineate, in subsequent chapters, what would constitute either an art of sex or its morality.

❄

Two theories about the nature of sex are worth mentioning at the outset. I find each of them suggestive but finally unacceptable. The first of these maintains that sexual desire is just an appetite, and similar to other appetites that human beings possess. In English we have no verb for sexuality that is a perfect equivalent of the verbs *to hunger* and *to thirst*. The verb *to desire* serves for occasions of wanting that may or may not be sexual, and *to lust* often has built into it a negative connotation that does not apply to hunger and thirst. Nonetheless I will use the words *desire* and *lust* as terms that represent whatever part of sex is at least comparable to the having of an appetite of any kind. The first theory holds that sexual desire or lust is primarily, and basically, appetitive.

This approach draws its plausibility from the fact that sexual impulse originates in a succession of physiological events, much as hunger and thirst do. In each case the organism undergoes characteristic tensions that are eliminated once the appetite has been satisfied. When we experience hunger or thirst, we crave objects that our body can appropriate in accordance with their ability to satisfy us—which is to say, their capacity to gratify our appetitive needs in a manner that conduces to enjoyable sensations of taste, touch, smell, and possibly sight or hearing. In evaluating a sex act, we may want to distinguish between the enjoyability of these different sense modalities and their ability to lessen the relevant tensions. In the case of hunger and thirst, we can possibly wonder whether nourishment is a consequence of satisfying those appetites or, instead, a criterion—one among others—for establishing the value of any satisfaction related to them. Nourishment is usually both, but if we think of it as crucial in the evaluation of eating or drinking, that militates against treating sex as an appetite comparable to these two. Sexuality does not nourish us in the sense in which eating and drinking do.

One could say that sexuality, as in reproductive coitus, is the result of a programmed drive that functions like a biological *analogue* to our search for nourishment. As eating and drinking provide nutrition we must have in order to survive, so too does coitus regenerate the species by conducing to its further existence. But obviously this equivalence does not hold. Only rarely does coitus result in reproduction, whereas eating and drinking constantly replenish the organism. The lusting that impels us to engage in sex acts can be satisfied an indefinite number of times, and throughout a lifetime, without ever benefiting the species. Feeling hunger or thirst is not analogous.

Sexual desire resembles hunger and thirst, and like them may be classified as an appetite, not only because it directly originates in a physiological mechanism but also because its tensions, like theirs, can be eliminated in ways that may involve no other human being. Whether or not masturbation can remove *all* of the tensions that are distinctly sexual, the fact remains that a gamut of them can be fully satisfied by this activity. In saying this, I am not subscribing to the sexological view that all orgasms are the same regardless of the type of stimulation and whether or not it results from interpersonal behavior. Even if that were true, there would still be obvious psychological differences between one experience of orgasm and another, and some of these differences may be related to the differences between masturbatory and nonmasturbatory response.

Despite all such disparity, however, one might argue that masturbation satisfies an appetite in the absence of other human beings just as eating and drinking often do. We could say this because there is a biological striving in each case that may be quieted without any immediate contact with other people. To this degree, the criteria for evaluating sex would not differ in principle from those that are appropriate for evaluating eating and drinking. Once we disregard considerations of nourishment, the nonsexual criteria mainly involve modes of lessening unwanted cravings through enjoyable means of doing so. We resolve these issues by citing particular foods or beverages that satisfy an organism such as ours. Whichever satisfy us better than others are deemed preferable. The same would apply to sex.

But we also recognize that people vary tremendously in their needs, their tastes, and their idiosyncratic selection of food or drink. If sex were a comparable appetite, one would have to conclude that since it is so diverse in itself there can hardly be universal criteria for its evaluation. This is not to deny that people with an orientation toward heterosexual coitus, let us say, might validly insist that for them some of its practices are more satisfying than others, or even that such practices are more satisfying for almost all people who do prefer heterosexual coitus. But it does mean that if someone reports that he or she enjoys sex that is homosexual rather than heterosexual, or masturbatory rather than coital, or bestial rather than human, we have no basis for thinking that these ways of gratifying sexual appetite are necessarily inferior. As long as a person is agreeably satisfied, his or her preferences would be inherently as justifiable as anyone else's.

What shall we say about this conception? I do not believe the theory is wholly mistaken about the nature of human sexuality. But I do think it is incomplete and cannot be accepted as it stands. It asserts not only that sex is an appetite, which is right, but also that sex is *nothing but* an appetite. Leaving aside the social amenities that accompany eating and drinking, one might say that these are only appetites. Yet that, too, is not entirely correct, since the foods we eat and the beverages we drink take on pervasive and important meaning that cannot be explained merely by their ability to pacify physiological drives. We live *with* our appetites, not solely by means of them or in accordance with their demands.

Still it is true that, by and large, eating and drinking are occasions—sometimes very elaborate or ceremonial and even ritualistic occasions—for the satisfying of appetites that could have been satisfied mechanically (for example, through intravenous feeding) but that we choose to invest with as many of the delights of civilization as possible. Though sex is also an appetite, and though it often occurs in settings that are primarily appetitive, it usually— and significantly among human beings—involves interpersonal concerns in a way that is different from appetites such as eating or drinking. As I will argue further in the following chapter, the being of other persons has a role in sexual experience that makes it *greatly* different.

This brings me to the second theory that I find suggestive though incomplete. On this view, sex acts are paradigmatically instances of mutual response between people whose desires are aroused by the fact that each is desiring the other.

If we assert that sex is in itself dependent upon this mutuality of desire, we deny that various activities that seem to be sexual responses are "really" or "truly" sexual. The man who makes love to a plastic figurine does not expect it to feel any reciprocal desire. He may even have bought it because he knows it cannot react as a living creature might and therefore will not interfere with his private fantasies. But even if the object of our attention is a person and we engage in coitus with that person, we can always act in a manner that defeats the possibility of mutual responsiveness. The other man or woman can be used as an instrumentality, as just a device for venting our feelings and satisfying our appetitive drive regardless of whether he or she is aroused. On this second theory, such nonmutual behavior would fail to include the interactive relation that defines the very nature of human sexuality.

Some of my doubts about this idea will appear when I discuss reciprocity as a criterion for the evaluation of sex acts. Here I would like to note that the view is too restrictive as a general characterization of sex that exists among human beings. For one thing the view limits sex to an arbitrary range of possibilities. By making mutuality definitive, it requires us to treat all nonreciprocal activities as in themselves sexually inferior, whereas they may only be inferior (and even that is always open to debate) in their social or personal consequences. We would have to know a great deal about men who make love to plastic figurines, and about fetishists in general, before we can be sure that the quality of their individual orgasm is less good or truly sexual in any fashion than what they would experience while embracing a real, live person whose desire is aroused by their desire and even responds simultaneously.

There are interpersonal goods that the latter situation includes and the former does not. But some of these goods are extraneous to the sex act itself, and the rest may be limited to mutual sex without being definitive of sexuality as a whole. The second theory does not mean to restrict sexual goodness only to occasions of mutuality. Rather it chooses these occasions as exemplars of what sex must be like in its entirety. To say that, however, is to neglect other activities that are clearly sexual and that some people perform without having a mutual relationship, and even by defeating its occurrence. Men and women who engage in fantasy or in solitary masturbation or in coitus that uses one's partner as a vehicle for selfish gratification may possibly lose out on many of the joys of sex. On the other hand, they may be savoring pleasures that mutual lovers do not experience and are hardly able to evaluate. We need a theory of sex that will recognize the place of reciprocity in much of sexuality without treating this special ingredient as a defining property.

I have spoken of mutual or reciprocal sex as the basis on which one could argue that sexuality is not merely an appetite. But since, at best, reciprocity can yield only one of the criteria for evaluation, perhaps I should have formulated my critique in terms that involve interpersonal responses of any sort, whether or not they are reciprocal. Even if sex is not explicable as mutual desire, its nature in human beings might be said to comprise one or another interpersonal relation that sets it apart from nonsexual appetites. We could then argue that the fetishist, the masturbator, and the person who engages in selfish manipulation is uniting him- or herself to other individuals in a circuitous manner that helps to relieve psychological tensions while gratifying physiological needs. Such people use a physical object, or their own body, or someone else's, in a putative communion that expresses feelings, attitudes, aspirations, hopes, fears that could be shown—if we knew the particulars well enough—to signify a hidden or imagined relationship with persons who matter in their lives.

Nor are these interpersonal factors only causal, as they could be in descriptions of why it is that people eat and drink as they do. In solitary, fetishistic, bestial, or wholly selfish sex acts, similar in this respect to the ones that involve mutual arousal, the structure and the quality of the experience are themselves a function of needs and desires that emanate from possible or actual relations to other human beings. In emphasizing this, the second theory, suitably modified, earns a place within an adequate definition of sex.

Despite their differences, the two theories I have been examining are compatible with each other. The idea of sex as appetite and the idea of sex as interpersonal bond are congruent, except when either claims to be exclusive. In its broad and most frequent range, sexuality is both interpersonal and appetitive. At the same time, we can imagine circumstances in which it might approach one or the other extreme. I am not ready to say that every occasion of orgasm must be interpersonal either directly or indirectly. Nocturnal emissions may sometimes be purely physiological, and even in the performance of masturbation we know that women seem to differ from men inasmuch as they more often stimulate themselves and release their sexual tension without fantasies or other obvious signs of interpersonal interest.

At the same time, we can also imagine a reciprocal relationship between people in whom (as often happens in later life) the appetite for sex has diminished greatly, almost entirely perhaps, although the partners engage in sexual behavior as a satisfying expression of their ongoing feelings about each other. These persons could hardly participate in sex without some of the residual appetite. But even so, it would be the interpersonality of their attachment that explains the nature of their sexual intimacy—and what matters in it—more than anything else.

The two coordinates, the appetitive and the interpersonal, may therefore serve as limiting conditions that jointly define human sexuality. To find the criteria that we might plausibly invoke for the evaluation of sex acts, we have to go beyond either of these coordinates taken in isolation from the other while also appreciating the many ways they interact. That will be my governing endeavor in the following chapters.

4

Criteria of
Sexual Goodness

Though I will be enumerating criteria for the
evaluation of sex, I do not pretend to be giving an
exhaustive list. Nevertheless the consecutive discussion
of these criteria, presented here without fixed claims
about their relative importance, can have its own utility. If
my effort succeeds, it may help to clarify the different
ways that sexuality can constitute a natural goodness in
human experience.

PLEASURE

Within the many dimensions of sex, pleasure has often
been considered the most obvious criterion of its
goodness. Apart from reproductive necessities, why else
would people engage in sexual experience and behavior
with the recurrent preoccupation that engulfs so much of
life in our species? As a first approximation, the idea that
pleasure is a motivating principle seems quite obvious.

But one is immediately confronted with problems about hedonic standards of value that are troublesome in several respects. These problems apply to human feeling as a whole, but philosophers have rarely studied them in terms of sexuality itself.

Hedonists like Bentham, Beccaria, Helvétius, and James Mill spoke of pleasure as if it were a sensation comparable to most others, localizable and even quantifiable. They seem to have thought it belongs to the same experiential spectrum as pain, occurring at the positive pole of a continuum in which pain is the negative opposite. Various critics have insisted that pleasure is not that sort of thing, and therefore that the hedonists are confused or mistaken. I myself have no intention of either defending hedonistic philosophy as it has been traditionally formulated or of rejecting it out of hand. Instead I wish to analyze the sense in which one might say that sexuality does involve pleasure of a special type. Knowing that, we can then decide whether this hedonic quality is a basis for understanding and evaluating sex acts.

To begin with, I believe that the hedonists are wrong, and their critics are right, if the former mean (as they sometimes do seem to mean) that when people talk about pleasure they generally have in mind a particular datum or state of being that yields an experience similar to, say, the experience of the color white that now exists in my visual field. The critics are wrong, however, if they think that there are no sensations that may be called "a pleasure" analogous to the way in which a visual sensation of white may be called "a color." Pleasures of this sort are possibly more intense in sexual experience than anywhere else in life. In developing their argument against traditional hedonism as persuasively as they do, its critics tend to disregard that and other facts of sexual phenomenology.

What we call the pleasure of a conversation, or doing carpentry, or strolling through the woods, may well occur without our having a sensation of pleasure that could be analyzed as separate from the activity of talking, planing a board, walking among the trees, or whatever it is we delight in. Our ability to carry out such pursuits with continuous and gratifying interest may be all or most of what one means in saying that they are pleasant or even pleasurable. Those terms mainly signify that the experience is welcome and quite acceptable. But in this regard sex is significantly different from other areas of life. It is a circumstance in which the body and all its senses are aroused, or at least stimulated, for the purpose of inducing specific and partly localized sensations that are hedonically charged.

I do not mean that in sex our senses are always aroused or stimulated for themselves alone, for the sake of nothing else. Though this often happens, it need not. Lovers and voluptuaries alike may linger upon the providing or receiving of pleasure, for instance by prolonged caressing of the genitals. For many couples this can even become the goal of lovemaking rather than being a preliminary stage in it. That happens among people who have a passion for the sensuous. But sexuality usually encompasses more than just the cultivation of explicit pleasure. Sex also lends itself to responses of a different and competing kind.

Gilbert Ryle argued that if there were such a thing as a sensation of pleasure that affects our experience and behavior, people who found some activity pleasurable would tend to be fixated upon the hedonic stimulus and never get on with the pleasurable event itself.[1] But even if this argument is convincing for specifiable interests one might have, there are numerous occasions of sexuality to which it simply does not apply. On these occasions people give themselves to conditions that are contrived for the creating of pleasurable qualities, discernible feelings of a positive character that are relished whether or not they deflect one from something beyond themselves.

As I will argue in the next section, we need to distinguish between sexual pleasure in this sense, as a particular sensation especially relevant to sex, and the having of a sexual experience that is only pleasant or enjoyable. The latter is unobtrusively hedonic in a way that can be illustrated by the examples I mentioned earlier—an engrossing conversation, or a cheerful doing of carpentry, or a felicitous stroll in the woods—as well as by sexual response.

In creating sensory pleasures that are not reducible to the mere enjoyability of an action, sex may be compared to arts such as music or painting. There, too, we often speak of sensations—in their case mainly sounds and sights—that give us pleasure in themselves. These art forms are nevertheless different from, and inferior to, sexuality as far as the sensation of pleasure is concerned. In making this point, and henceforth in my argument, I use the word *pleasure* to refer to the separate and explicit datum in hedonic consciousness. I employ the terms *enjoyment* or *pleasantness* to signify the agreeable tone that pervades experiences we find gratifying whether or not they yield distinct and determinate sensations of pleasure. Music, for instance, can give great enjoyment, very often greater enjoyment than in sex, but rarely does it provide pleasure of the type that most people value and pursue through sexual encounters.

Of course, we may speak of a bel canto voice making "ear-ravishing" sounds, and the fact that this metaphor is somewhat sexual might encourage us to think that these sounds afford pleasures comparable to the exquisite sensations that lovers feel in being kissed on the lips or tickled on the inner thigh. But the auditory experience is generically different from the sexual feeling. Aural excitation is incapable of creating pleasures in the way that tactile stimulation does, except perhaps on those occasions when hearing reverberates throughout the body. If one thrills to a trumpet blast or the pounding of drums, or even certain forceful dissonances in the orchestra, one may sometimes have a sensation of pleasure that approximates the tactile and kinesthetic sensations that sex can readily evoke. In music as we have known it in the Western world, however, these sensations are fairly uncommon, and normally associated with effects that we consider vulgar or uninspired if they do not contribute to more extensive aesthetic enjoyment in the art form.

When a soprano sings with great bravura and agility, making astounding leaps or runs that cause our spine to tingle quite literally, we could say that she has given pleasure in the narrower sense. But to assert that her singing is ear-ravishing means something else: namely, that hearing it provides a sense of happiness or well-being, resulting perhaps from the delicacy and purity of her voice rather than its ability to arouse pleasure as a localized sensation.

This difference between sex and arts like music or painting may be related to the fact that these media are not inherently tactile. But I think it is significant that only in sex does one have hedonic experiences that use a combination of senses instead of concentrating upon any one exclusively. Even if the sense of touch has greater and more focused power to instill pleasure than hearing or sight, sexuality augments our capacity for tactile pleasures by enlisting the cooperation of these other acuities as well.

Lovemaking in general appropriates the ordinary functions of faculties that enable us to perceive another human being, employing them not only for the sake of some visual or sonic enjoyment that may occur in painting or music, but also as instrumentalities for the creation of tactile pleasures. These are further heightened in their intensity by being associated with moments of increased emotionality that make us more alert to the possibilities of touch. Sometimes the reverse may also happen, for sensitivity to touching and being touched can diminish if one is in the throes of extreme passion. Such is the price one pays for passing far beyond the wholly sensuous. But before this occurs, sexuality usually creates a lesser though mounting level of excitement or emotional involvement commensurate with our ability to feel the pleasures of tactile stimulation.

Above all when it is strongly felt, sexual pleasure may induce elements of pain. The nineteenth-century hedonists were mistaken in thinking that pleasure and pain are polar opposites. Each is a sensation, each can be localized, and if one follows upon the other, it may seem as though white has turned into black or an affirmative has been changed into a negative. But in sexual experience pleasure is intermingled with tension, discomfort, strain, and perhaps a vivid feeling of pain which, when they are not too acute, yield a pleasure in themselves. In sex pure pleasures can occur, if they occur anywhere in life, but the nature of affective arousal and bodily contact is such that most sexual pleasures are impure: they include components that are not entirely pleasurable. That is most obvious in passionate sex, whose pains as well as pleasures are often stronger than even the excruciating joy of sensuous sex.

SEX: A PHILOSOPHICAL PRIMER

This fact has encouraged moralists across the ages to vilify human sexuality, and to do so, I think, by means of a verbal trick that sometimes borders on intellectual dishonesty. Since sexual pleasure is frequently mixed or impure, even great philosophers like Plato and Lucretius have reached the non sequitur of concluding that sex is impure in a normative or spiritual sense. One could, however, argue that the redeeming virtue of sexuality consists in its capacity—possibly unique in our being—to render a great variety of physical and emotional cravings, involving material and psychological tensions, into an agency for pleasurable experience that not only alleviates their distressfulness but actually transforms them into experiential patterns so affirmatively desirable as to make our impure and imperfect existence emphatically worth living.

Being something people cherish and cultivate, something men and women seek in their extraordinary efforts to do whatever may foster it, pleasure is one of the most important criteria for the evaluation of sex acts. Everything else being equal, one must believe that if some event gives more pleasure than another, then the first one has to be considered better to that extent. There may be reasons to avoid behavior that is highly pleasurable, and doubtless they can account for the fact that most societies have repressed sexuality and philosophers have all too often warned us about the dangers of what they disparagingly call "passion." But if anything is so, the mere existence of pleasure is surely evidence of goodness in the sex acts themselves.

At the same time, we might find it difficult to gauge the relative goodness of equally pleasurable sex acts. Criteria other than pleasure must also be introduced, and I, for one, doubt that we really know what it means to say that different sex acts can be "equally pleasurable." How would we compare them in order to decide whether or not they are quantifiably the same? We can perceive the difference between their pleasurability if one of them definitely yields pleasure while the other is painful or just boring. But what shall we say about occasions that differ in the duration, strength, and relative ranking of their individual pleasures? In our hedonic calculus, are we to assume that pleasures can be added, or should they be multiplied? If a pleasure is very powerful but short-lived, does it count as more pleasurable than one that is less intense but has greater endurance?

The problem seems irresolvable, and possibly verbal since it may depend upon the ambiguous meaning of the word *more* in this peculiar usage. For additional insight we need to go beyond the criterion of pleasure alone. And we should always be mindful of what Saint-Preux says in Rousseau's *La Nouvelle Héloïse*. After having had ecstatic sexual intercourse with Julie, the woman he loves, Saint-Preux remarks that the subsequent memories of their lovemaking were even sweeter than what he felt during the act itself.

ENJOYMENT AND SATISFACTION

Though it sometimes happens, we rarely engage in an activity for the sake of nothing but the pleasures it affords. One can imagine a person passionately devoting him- or herself to a search for pleasures, as one can imagine people spending their time and energy looking for gall wasps. Kinsey collected four million specimens of gall wasps, and we may assume that there have been libertines who managed to savor a great multitude of different sexual pleasures, whether or not they classified them into species and accumulated them with scientific devotion. This kind of interest, like the obsession that motivates a Kinsey, is exceptional. It is a special taste, in no way definitive of human sexuality. Most people, above all those who seek to refine the aesthetic capabilities of sex, dedicate themselves to affective goods that are not reducible to pleasure. Undesirable or evil as it is, pain does not dominate our entire existence to a degree that would allow us to believe that people avoid it throughout their lives. Similarly, pleasure—good as it may be—is not an invariable object of pursuit, even on the part of those who consider themselves hedonists.

I have been using the word *enjoyment* to specify a positive hedonic tone that differs from pleasure in being a pervasively agreeable quality in experience, rather than something that demarcates a separate and identifiable sensation. I shall presently distinguish between enjoyment and satisfaction, which is also hedonic and also different from pleasure. But first I would like to point out that enjoyment, unlike pleasure, need not be physical. The words *pleasure* and *pain* do refer, on some occasions of their use, to conditions that are metaphorically nonphysical. In *My Fair Lady*, Professor Higgins complains of people whose English is painful to one's ears, and a lover might declare that his sweetheart's smile is a pleasure to behold. But these figurative expressions should not fool us into thinking that pleasure or pain can *literally* be anything other than material occurrences resulting from direct sensory excitation. For us to *enjoy* anything, however, our experience need only consist of gratifying qualities, none of which have to be physical either literally or metaphorically. A man who is pleasuring a woman in sexual intercourse gives her pleasures in the strict sense of that word, but he himself may experience simply the enjoyment of knowing that his amatory efforts are succeeding.

One might remark that the word *simply* is inaccurate here, since (as a matter of fact, to be established independently) people do not ordinarily enjoy knowing that they are giving pleasure unless their physical gestures—the actual means by which the giving occurs— are enjoyable in themselves. But even so, that would only mean that people may be impeded from giving pleasure if they do not enjoy what needs to be done for that purpose. This empirical generalization does not explain the enjoyment that men and women can feel in *knowing* about the consequences of their involvement. And in any event, enjoying the ability to use one's body to create pleasure in another is quite different from getting pleasure oneself from the requisite behavior.

In sexuality, much of what we loosely call "the cultivating of pleasure," or "the indulging in pleasure," and so forth, really pertains to the possibilities of enjoyment rather than pleasure. Sexuality can relate us to each other in ways that evoke psychological unity or oneness, emotional corroboration and support, a sense of security, and a wide spectrum of desired feelings none of which may be so distinct or localized as to be called a pleasure. The hedonic goods I have just cited are types of enjoyment that belong to sex at its best. In all epochs of history, and in every society, human beings have cherished the situations that bring them into being.

These moments of enjoyment, and others that we can easily imagine, are not entirely gratuitous. They do not drop upon us by chance, and neither do they occur through a relaxation of our concern about other people, or the world of communality these people establish through their association with us. For this reason philosophers are naive when they speak of sex as a turning away from interpersonal attitudes. Not only is sexual enjoyment often benevolent and altruistic, each individual being happy to afford what the other desires, but also the participants must learn how to enjoy the act of relating to this other man or woman under the interpersonal conditions afforded by sexuality. That would not be the case if the activities were an escape from social awareness. Such statements about the nature of sex make it sound trivial and superficial, or worse, a delectable titillation perhaps but a disposition that has nothing to do with compassionate love or fellow feeling.

It would be more accurate, I suggest, to say that the hedonic attributes of viable sexuality tell us a great deal about human fulfillment and the satisfaction of our fundamental needs. I introduce the concept of satisfaction here not to replace the criterion of enjoyment but to supplement it with a somewhat overlapping notion. What we enjoy usually results from attaining something that satisfies organic drives and whatever desires are derivative from them.

The relationship between enjoyment and satisfaction is most apparent in conduct that is clearly appetitive. Eating and drinking are enjoyable because, for the most part, they satisfy our need for food and fluids. But also one could distinguish between the enjoyment of a banquet in the company of people we like and the level of satisfaction that comes from the meal itself. We might claim that men and women have a need for human companionship, but we could not say (except as a witticism) that anyone has a need for banquets. If the latter are enjoyable, their enjoyability is therefore distinguishable from satisfactions without which this form of enjoyment would not exist. Conversely the criterion of satisfaction serves as an additional coordinate by which we may judge the goodness of all types of experience or behavior.

Since sex is an interpersonal appetite, its satisfactions involve needs that often exceed the material or physiological urgencies related to reproductive responses. Unless there were some genital impulse, however meager, one might want to deny that a relationship is truly sexual. But even where someone's craving for another person depends on libidinal drive, it is not reducible to that alone. In needing other people, we also need them as a means for expressing social and interpersonal feelings in the most intimate connection possible. The activation of the genitals, and the contact between parts of the body that we are not allowed to touch in the more casual relations of daily life, creates the opportunity for such intimacy. The purely physical is thus an impetus that helps to explain the causation of sex but not its total being.

A society in which everyone freely fondled everyone else—as chimpanzee males do when they investigate the pudenda of any female who happens to be in the vicinity—might turn out to be a society that lacks a sense of sexual intimacy. In that event, it would be hard for us to get the kind of satisfaction that either the sensuous or the passionate provides. In a world in which people developed to adulthood without any social interaction, a world in which the young sprang from an egg full grown (as they do in Shaw's *Back to Methuselah*), a world in which there was no process of psychodynamic maturation beginning with total dependence upon a parental figure followed by a gradual and tortuous emancipation that never ends—in such a world, assuming that we have not so greatly changed the nature of what it is to be a human being that our idea renders speculation utterly fruitless, there would be no need for either sexual intimacy or the completion of interpersonal desires by means of it.

Emotional as well as physical satisfaction is a criterion for the goodness or badness of sex acts because the world we inhabit is not like that one.

As a criterion of evaluation, satisfaction ranges across the multiple interests that might be gratifiable in any one experience. In being both appetitive and interpersonal, desires that enter into sex are often incommensurable. The orgasm yields satisfying release of tensions that permeate the entire body although they are felt most keenly in the genitals. The tensions as well as their relief are often devices artificially produced, since sexual stimulation itself may cause a person to be aroused to a pitch of excitement that he or she would not have felt in any other circumstance. Throughout the years of maturity, however, people often seem to be in a state of latent arousability. It is as if genital and libidinal tensions exist just beneath the surface of our organic condition, sometimes leading to erotic and romantic behavior whether or not the underlying forces appear in consciousness. They frequently occur in a mechanical fashion and accompanied by little awareness of who or what may have brought them into being.

For the most part, a failure to ease such tensions eventuates in a sense of dissatisfaction that is not only frustrating to the individual but also prevents him or her from enjoying other aspects of life. In an obvious sense, good sex is sexual experience that allows someone to attain satisfactions of any sort that may result from the elimination of sex-related tensions. Whether one sex act is superior to another because it creates tensions and then relieves them, whereas the other merely releases tensions that existed antecedently, is a question we need not consider.

Similarly, we need not determine whether it is preferable to satisfy sexual desires by means of orgasmic experience rather than some other way that people might find more feasible, and even more enjoyable. At the present stage of sexological science, no one knows enough about the nature of sex to analyze it so minutely that we can be sure either that orgasms are essential for quieting sexual tensions or that other types of response may make it unnecessary for sexual satisfaction to occur by means of the orgasm. We know that orgasms tender a recognizable form of satisfaction. But for all we can tell, nonorgasmic satisfactions may sometimes be more desirable, more conducive to the goodness of good sex.[2] The criterion of satisfaction ascribes badness to the occurrence of frustration, unwanted tension, and a persistent restlessness that clogs the sexual membranes of one's life. That may be all that one can say reliably.

COMPLETENESS AND RECIPROCITY

Completeness is a criterion that philosophers have sometimes used for the evaluation of sex acts, but they generally interpret it as more or less synonymous with reciprocity. In the context of my earlier remarks about mutual desire, I will separate reciprocity from completeness and treat them as different criteria.

It is important to distinguish between completeness and reciprocity because a complete relationship can exist without there being any arousal of responsive desires. Moreover, completeness involves conditions that are not the same as in the experience of reciprocal desire. All such terminology is ambiguous, of course, but one of the things that people generally mean by completeness is the fact that a sexual event satisfies in what the sexologists call a "terminative" manner. That signifies that, for a while at least, sexual tension disappears. Reciprocity alone gives no assurance that either of the participants will be fully satisfied, and no guarantee that whatever satisfactions are attained will bring a termination of sexual craving.

The criterion of completeness-as-termination goes beyond the idea of satisfaction alone inasmuch as it specifies a *total* satisfaction that a sex act can yield in and by itself. The distinction between satisfaction and complete quiescence is worth making because women, in particular, are capable of orgasms that may be said to satisfy them although they often belong to a multiple series within which even the final orgasm is not wholly satisfying. Many women report that they could, and would like to, go on having orgasms but stop out of fatigue. This does not indicate a lack of satisfaction in the orgasms that these multiorgasmic women do experience, nor is there anything necessarily inferior in their pattern of response. But if each experience is such that by itself it feels incomplete or is less than wholly satisfying, in the sense that the women desire additional orgasms, there must be a kind of sexual goodness that eludes them and that their responsiveness does not illustrate.

A complete satisfaction, a satisfaction or system of satisfactions that gives a feeling of completeness in a sex act, would release tensions and afford pleasures or enjoyments that bring sexual activity to an end for reasons apart from mere fatigue or absence of stimulation. A sexual experience is complete when the person is drained of sexual impulse for a significant time afterward. It is a state of being that Brahms portrays, beyond any words that I could summon, in his love song "*Gestillte Sehnsucht*" (Quieted Longing). Courbet's great painting "*Le Sommeil*" (Sleep), which depicts two naked and fulfilled young women slumbering blissfully in each other's arms, celebrates a similar consummation as the possible outcome of lesbian sexuality.

A comparable completeness—though not always as emotionally intense—is routine among orgasmic males, most of whom experience a refractory period of a few or even many minutes during which it is difficult for them to have a further erection. The interlude results from a resolution in the previous sex act that is not only good in itself but also one of the criteria for goodness. Satisfied as he may otherwise be, the male might consider his orgasm imperfect or substandard unless it were complete in this sense.

Since many women are not interested in completeness, the contrary mode of satisfaction often being the one they prefer, it can hardly be considered a universal criterion. Even among the males, little boys sometimes manifest multiorgasmic (though nonejaculatory) behavior that resembles the female pattern in lacking a refractory period. It would be unreasonable to assume that their experience must be deficient just because it is incomplete.

One might argue that if completeness is not a universal criterion it is not a criterion at all. It might just be one of the goods that sex can sometimes offer. If so, it would not serve as a basis for evaluating different sex acts. Thus far I have not approached the question of how these criteria are to be used. I first want to list and analyze them. We can later determine what their moral economy must be.

Philosophers who identify completeness with reciprocity tend to neglect the importance of terminativeness (and even satisfaction). They emphasize the arousing of desires in a mutual and reflexive manner even though this does not indicate that either partner will ever be satisfied. When Thomas Nagel defines the completeness of a "full-fledged sexual relation" in terms of a desire that someone be aroused by merely recognizing another person's desire to arouse him or her, he seems unconcerned about the fact that completeness in the sex act requires more than just this mutuality of reciprocal arousal. Nagel may possibly think of reciprocity as only a necessary condition for completeness; but even then, it seems strange to claim that the release of sexual energy cannot be complete without the ricochet of desires specified by Nagel's theory.[3]

We may also question whether reciprocity is in fact a necessary condition. As Nagel presents it, the mutual arousal sounds like an interest that some people do have but that men and women often find quite dispensable. There is something very cerebral, and oddly distanced, in being stimulated by the realization that our partner has a desire to stimulate us. Sara Ruddick and others improve Nagel's analysis by eliminating the idea that each participant must be aroused by a reciprocal desire to arouse. These philosophers argue that what is truly arousing is not another's desire to arouse but rather his or her desire for sexual enjoyment, or else his or her desire for oneself.[4]

But here, too, in this simplified and more plausible formulation, we may wonder whether any mutuality is paradigmatic for the responses that different people experience in the varied conditions we ordinarily consider sexual. Inasmuch as intercourse requires at least two participants, we might say that the sexuality binding them must depend upon feelings and desires each has in relation to the other. But is it *essential* that these feelings and desires be aroused by a reciprocating affect in the other person?

There is an undeniable excitement and organic beauty that issues from mutual response throughout a sexual encounter, one person's gestures initiating an immediate reaction, every reaction eliciting some resonant demonstration of feeling, the intertwining bodies, emotions, personalities reverberating within a continuous ricochet of intense expressiveness. This alone reveals the possibilities of consummation in human sexuality, as it would (with modifications) in the performing of ensemble music, or a fervent discussion, or even a vigorous exchange of hostility. The brawls that occur so frequently in hockey games (or Hollywood movies) have in them elements that are kindred to sexual reciprocity.

The oneness that eventuates from this conjunction of disparate vitalities, each attuned to the other despite their differences, can very well prefigure a kind of love that we will presently discuss. But however magnificent the enactment of sexual reciprocity may be, assuming it is accompanied by an appropriate mode of satisfaction, we should not conclude that enjoyable, pleasurable, or satisfying sex must be inferior *as sex* whenever reciprocity does not exist.

For one thing, reciprocity of any sort is not definitive statistically. It often occurs but probably less often than the joint but nonreciprocal discharge of desire. Both participants may feel sexual yearning at the same time and within the same session of lovemaking. Yet each may direct his or her drive toward the other without needing to be aroused by a reactive feeling that emanates from this person. For people who have been reared to think that there is something wrong about sexuality as a whole, or that something terribly dangerous resides within the everpresent possibility of frustration, it can be very stimulating (as well as flattering) to see that a man or woman who awakens our physical desire has a comparable interest in us. Such corroboration, which may look like authorization, furthers our own arousal. It encourages in us hopes of imminent happiness. But that is not a prerequisite for even successful sex.

Sexual impulse is often elicited by the sheer loveliness of a person's face or figure, and occasionally by his or her resemblance to someone else we care about. The fact that a man or woman has been sexually aroused in relation to us may have little or no effect upon our own arousability. Even rock stars and movie idols are not that vain. As a defining principle in the analysis of sex, reciprocity is both too narrow and too strong, despite the fact that awareness of the other person's desire may on occasion cause us to desire him or her.

Over and above questions about the nature of reciprocity, we may also wonder whether joint occurrence of desire—which is more likely to happen—can serve as a suitable criterion for either defining or evaluating sexuality. Both Nagel and Ruddick believe that a complete sex act involves two participants who are, and must be, responsive at the same time. But why impose this restriction? Why must each have sexual feelings when the other does? Human beings are not geared and synchronized so precisely that partners, even in a perfect marriage, will always have identical or similar interests.

There is an efficiency of emotional energy that results from a nice coordination among the desires and satisfactions people can possibly experience when they live together in an intimate relationship. Everything else being equal, one might say that this is preferable to any alternative. But everything else never is equal in this respect, since human sexuality interacts with other regions of life that often command immediate attention.

These competing vectors can prevent two persons from responding to each other in a neatly integrated and well-attuned fashion. If one participant is sexually aroused but the other is not, the one who is aroused may take the frigidity of the other as a sign of indifference and latent anger. This painful inference would not occur, however, if they recognized that sexual impulse evades the control of those who either have or fail to have it. When people are sufficiently secure in a sexual situation, they realize that even love may often be unable to call forth desire.

The view that considers mutuality of arousal essential for completeness suffers from an inadequacy of description. In suggesting that reciprocal desire reveals the basic framework of sexuality, this type of approach ignores the fact that our desire can be created not only by responsiveness to the other person's desire for us, but also by the mere awareness that he or she is in a desiring mode. This shows itself in behavior unrelated to our desire which manifests his or her separate need to get the pleasure, enjoyment, or satisfaction that issues from intimate relations. The bodily or linguistic signals of this can augment our own sexual appetites. But adequate stimulation may also be quite mechanical, and solitary masturbators may frequently use their imagination to attain something more or less equivalent to interpersonal gratification.[5]

LOVE

If love were a specific sensation or emotion, one might say that sex acts accompanied by this desirable feeling are better than those that occur without it. But there is no single entity, no discernible sensation or emotion, that is love, as Wittgenstein also remarks. There is no feeling, no unique and explicit datum, such that love exists if and only if it is present.[6] Love is a form of life, though often short-lived, a disposition, a tendency to respond in a great variety of ways, many overlapping but none that is necessary and sufficient. It is a propensity to have affirmative and corroborative responses, thoughts, and inclinations to act without being limited to any one paradigmatically. That pluralistic assumption pervades my attempt to define love in terms of valuational concepts such as appraisal and what I call bestowal. These signify attitudes, affective orientations, that show themselves in different feelings, predilections, proclivities, and diversified judgments as well as sensations or emotions.[7]

If love is useless for the evaluation of sex acts as long as we think of it as an isolatable something, we may nevertheless believe that the broader conception of love can possibly yield a suitable criterion. On the other hand, we might argue that even though love is a virtue and achievement to which good sex conduces there is no justification for defining sexuality itself in terms of love. In that eventuality, love would not be a basis for gauging the value of different sex acts. On this view, the most one could say is that people who respond to each other in the ways that result in sexual goodness are likely to be people who love each other. Where sex fails, it becomes difficult for men and women to achieve the positive union that love involves. Conversely, love might be seen as a state that generally facilitates the occurrence of good sex without being in itself a criterion of what is good in sex.

Leaving aside for the moment this problem about love as a criterion of sexual goodness, one could argue that both of the empirical generalizations I have mentioned are unconvincing. We can easily imagine people who love each other without feeling desires that would enable their love to express itself sexually. We can also imagine people who have sex experiences that are extremely good, since they meet evaluative criteria such as satisfaction or pleasure or enjoyment to a remarkable degree, without there being love between the partners as a preliminary or sustaining condition for the existence of their sexual success. The question is whether these circumstances in which love has no uniform relation to good sex are frequent and statistically normal. It is not enough just to *imagine* good sex independent of any previous or subsequent love. One has to know what is likely, and even very probable. But here we are faced by the fact that human beings are so different, and their sex acts so variable among themselves, that the causal ties between love and sexuality may well involve too many unknowns for us to reach any justifiable conclusion.

In some societies men visit prostitutes, or temple harlots, or one or another of many wives, in order to attain physical gratification that is designed to have no connection with love, or hardly any. In other societies, it is difficult for some men, and very often women as well, to function sexually in even the most limited manner unless they are propelled toward someone by mutual love that makes them feel a sense of commitment that the other person conveys through her or his sexuality. Good sex may conduce to love for another person, as any type of proffered goodness would. But the nature of this benign interaction is complex and needs to be clarified.

What we really want to know is whether love within a sex act can ever count as a criterion for evaluation. Regardless of why it is that a man visits a prostitute or temple harlot, and regardless of the marital cohesiveness that good sex between husband and wife may create in them, one can possibly say that sexual behavior enacted with love is inherently superior whenever it occurs. Though a man may not love a woman, or vice versa, before their sexual conjunction, they might nevertheless find that their relationship is more satisfying and more enjoyable if they feel love for each other in the act of *making* love.

Under these conditions the criterion for evaluation would still be satisfaction or enjoyment rather than love. But since many people cannot operate sexually apart from love, we might infer that love bears so close a relationship to sexuality that the sheer occurrence of love makes a sex act better. Its absence in situations where two people feel indifferent toward each other we would interpret as a diminution of the quality of a sexual encounter. And though sex, even good sex, is entirely compatible with feelings of anger and even hatred, we might argue that unless some elements of love were also present on such occasions the sexual experience would not be enjoyable or satisfying. Though sadists and masochists may experience sex that is good, inasmuch as it gives them considerable gratification, their sexuality too may be permeated by some kind of twisted love as well as cruelty and self-abnegation. Their pathology consists in the way in which the negative components are dominant rather than being harnessed by the love they cannot negotiate successfully.

In suggesting that love may be a criterion for good sex, not only a value to which good sex leads or just a state out of which good sex emanates, I am aware that love can be unrequited. A person may use sex as a means of expressing love toward someone who may or may not feel love in return. At times in the Western world when marriages were arranged by the families, women were encouraged to accept a man whom they would someday come to love despite the fact that they did not love him at the beginning of their married life. One can well imagine that loving husbands tried to nurture love as well as desire by means of sexual endearments. Until this succeeded, there would not have been any reciprocity of love. We also know that pleasure, enjoyment, or satisfaction often remain one-sided in sex. But if a sex act issues from mutual love, is it not *inherently* preferable to one that fails in that respect?

Where mutual love exists, each person is concerned about the welfare, the feelings, and the indefeasible needs that make the other whatever he or she is. What matters to one, matters to both, not by chance or coincidence but simply *because* it matters to that other person. Something the woman cares about, the result of an election for instance, may only matter to the man in the sense that he cares about what matters to her, not because he himself has any interest in who wins the election. If only in this indirect way, the feelings of each (and probably their cognitive orientations as well) change in accordance with the affective responses of the other person. If this kind of interaction is recurrent in their life together, it could increase the goodness of their sexual experience. To say, then, that mutual love serves as a criterion for the goodness of sex acts would be to specify a condition that is more than just the individual love or sexual impulse of either participant alone. Are we prepared to go that far?

Compared with criteria such as the experience of pleasure, which is graphic and unmistakable when it occurs, love is extremely vague and sometimes imperceptible. But the advent of love, often when it is one-sided but above all when it is mutual, makes so great a difference in the quality of sexual encounters that we may well list it as a major criterion. If sex were nothing but an appetite, the love of another human being might operate only peripherally in sexual consummation, the way that a love of food does in the satisfying of hunger. But since sex is also interpersonal, it depends upon love as that which expresses our valuational bestowal upon an individual we cherish and respect. He or she exists for us as someone to whom we can truly relate, and perhaps as a living reality whom we would not even desire if there were no abiding love that makes a unity of us. Love gives sexual events a meaningfulness that does not come into being otherwise.

From this point of view, sexual love is the realization of that much in sex which is ideally interpersonal. Love is the means by which the appetitiveness of sexuality becomes transformed as the valued vehicle of interpersonal goodness. It follows that love is rightly considered a criterion for the evaluation of sex acts. Whether or not it is mutual, love constitutes a basic motive *within* human sexuality.[8]

EMBODIMENT AND ABSORPTION

The criteria I have listed thus far may not be exhaustive, and further investigation might disclose that some of them can be analyzed into components that ought to stand as separate criteria on their own. For instance, there may be a sense of the word *respect* such that no love can exist unless partners respect each other. Having analyzed love and discovered this essential ingredient, we might wish to infer that respect is a criterion for evaluating sex acts whether or not respect amounts to love.

In a similar vein we could think of compassion as a relevant criterion. If compassion is internally related to both sex and love, as I suggested in the first chapter of this book, we might conclude that the intrinsic value of sexual experience depends not only on interpersonal love in general but also on the type of love that is compassion. We could then see human sexuality as, in part, a reaching out for physical oneness with someone whose plight in life we recognize and want to ameliorate through active involvement.

At present I will content myself with treating love as a criterion without delving into its subsidiary implications. Too much discussion of components like respect or compassion might deflect us from appreciating love's continuity with the other criteria I have listed. Pleasure, enjoyment, satisfaction, completeness, and love itself—all of which may or may not be mutual but any of which can exist in relation to someone else—make up a unified class of affective attachments present in sexual intimacy of every sort. They each depend upon the fact that sex in human beings is appetitive as well as personal in varying degrees. They each pertain to both the sensuous and the passionate. They each have pervasive importance since they exist in different, sometimes vastly different, types of sexual behavior and can therefore have the kind of generality needed to explain both the nature and evaluation of sex acts.

In contrast to these criteria of good or better sex, there are conditions that have sometimes been suggested that I now want to reject as inappropriate. One of these is called "embodiment" (and sometimes "incarnation") by Sartre, Merleau-Ponty, and other existentialist thinkers. For them sex is the means by which consciousness becomes flesh. They define authentic sexuality as the state in which the embodiment of our consciousness through appetitive awareness of another person's flesh enables us to communicate with the consciousness of that other person, who is reflexively being embodied through his or her comparable awareness of our flesh.[9]

Aside from the obscurity of this conception of embodiment, I find it logically unstable. It presupposes a primordial split between consciousness and flesh, between mind and body, which sex presumably seeks to overcome. But the "overcoming" merely involves an awareness expressed in the form of sexual desire, as opposed to a detached observation or cool recognition that another person appears before us. What makes the difference between consciousness unembodied and consciousness embodied would seem to be only the occurrence of desire itself. If this is true, however, we have scarcely found an explanation of human sexuality or provided an analysis that can generate criteria for evaluation. It is quite trivial to say that sexual desire is a necessary condition for sex. If that is all we mean by embodiment, it cannot tell us much about the nature of sexuality. Nor can it count as a criterion for good or better sex.

As against my criticism, one might say that when Sartre and the others speak of embodiment they designate a state of absorption or boundless physical attraction, the consciousness of people becoming flesh inasmuch as they give themselves totally to their carnal interest in one another. No aspect of our being is then withheld, and we do not fix our attention upon ourselves or the parameters of our own existence. To say this would be to say that absorption alone can serve as a definition of sex. When we are distracted or fantasizing, or allow our thoughts to wander, we would not be having an experience that reveals the possibility of a relation in which we focus upon the sexuality of either ourselves or some other person. One might even claim that sexual absorption erases the separation between consciousness and flesh by preventing anything in them from intruding upon our full awareness of what we are and what the other is. Our conscious being cannot be alienated from our bodily condition once we become absorbed in a truly sexual encounter.

I find this argument unconvincing. Interpreting embodiment as absorption does not enable us to consider it a criterion of value. The absorbed state is a somewhat bizarre event. It cannot be considered paradigmatic for all of sex, or even all good sexuality. Is it intrinsically better to be carried away by a heightened level of excitation? Some people think so, and many adore the moments in which their passion has swept them into a blurring of their sense of separateness. But passionate extravagance of this type is not the only kind of sexual goodness, and the goodness of mindless abandon or emotional ecstasy cannot militate against the fact that calm and sensuous delectation may contribute pleasures or satisfactions that are equally fundamental in sex. Since these require an absence of absorption, I cannot believe that the more it exists, the better our sexual experience must be.

At one extreme we can cite limiting cases of schizophrenic withdrawal that are so greatly noninterpersonal, and even nonappetitive, as to suggest that a lack of absorption has impaired the ability of these people to be adequately sexual. But similarly we could maintain that someone so greatly absorbed as to pass out of consciousness and into blissful oblivion is also exceeding the bounds of sexuality. Within this range, demarcated by too little absorption at one pole and too much at the other, there resides an infinite variety in the ways that different people may be said to embody their consciousness. What is good or bad about any level of absorption will depend upon criteria such as pleasure or satisfaction. But these can be operative at virtually all the stages of positive response.

It is also possible that philosophers who treat absorption as a criterion of value mean only that a participant is not casual about his or her sexual behavior, as a man would be who worked on his income tax mentally while, in a detached manner, his pelvis massages his wife through penile thrusting. One often hears about women aimlessly eating an apple or reading a book or planning dinner while a man uses their body to gratify his lust. Surely such experience is less valuable as sex than when people respond to the embodied being of each other. But this is only to say that sexual relations are better for both persons if there is sexual feeling in each of them. There cannot be the satisfaction of desire, which we have already listed as a criterion for evaluation, unless there is an actual desire. And neither can pleasure or enjoyment exist unless we are presently immersed in the process of satisfying our desire.

Some thinkers doubt that any sexuality can be good without total absorption because they assume that a sex act must be deficient if one of the participants indulges in sexual fantasies. But this too may be an event that varies greatly among people whose sexual experience is equally authentic or consummatory. It is not at all clear that the woman who responds passionately to her husband of many years while also conjuring up an image of Cary Grant or Mel Gibson is thereby making her involvement in sex less good than it would have been without that image. One might say that she is not *really* responding to her husband, and so her relation to him is not the kind that love entails. But to know whether this opinion can be correct, we would need to have quite a bit more information about the woman's feelings toward her husband. If in fact she has no desire for him, but only for the movie star, to whom, alas, she does not have access, then there is definitely a lack of love to that extent, as evidenced by her deceptive attitude.

If, however, she uses her fantasy as a means of awakening in herself desire that she directs toward her husband, accepting him as the recipient if not the instigator of it, the imaginative performance she enacts may be a way of bestowing love upon him. Though the intervention of fantasies can signify diminished love between the spouses, it may also be a means of sharing beneficial satisfactions. It then functions as an expression of their love within a wholesome sexual situation. There is no reason to exclude sexual fantasies in advance.

The presence of such imagery in sex does not differ substantially from other inducements to sexual desire. A man or woman who has been excited by a photograph or a glimpse of someone in the street, or a remembrance of things past, may reasonably turn to an available partner in the hope that this lingering happenstance can bring satisfaction through physical contact with him or her as the person with whom one is intimately bonded at the moment. If the partner is used primarily as a body grafted onto the prior experience that engendered one's desire, the sexual event may well be inferior in itself and possibly inimical to love. But if the arousal directly contributes to explicit interest in the person we are having sex with, it no longer matters that our desire grew out of a situation that did not initially involve this man or woman. For that matter, who can say where any impulse originates? The fantasy that elicits our excitement is in principle no different from the hormonal or physiological forces that create one's sexual craving, whether or not we have a fantasy. The crucial question is how we use our feelings and casual images.

But now consider the case in which the sexual fantasy, even if it is fleeting and awakens a desire that directs itself to a partner whom we love, centers about a friend we often meet rather than a celebrity we have only seen as an image on the silver screen. There may be reason to think that revealing the identity of this other person would cause the partner to become jealous, or at least hurt, to some degree. And would not our interpersonal experience be threatened by his or her reaction? Though all is kept secret, the mere presence of another person in our thoughts—a real person, not just an idol—might affect our capacity for love and desired satisfaction in the immediate relationship with the man or woman to whom we are only partly attending. In that event, and to that extent, our sexual experience would be impaired.

Since sex is more than just appetitive, everything that prevents us from responding to and with our partner can jeopardize an extensive class of possible gratifications. But human beings are very resilient in these circumstances, and it would be foolish to think that the damage is always irredeemable.

NATURAL AND UNNATURAL

In the judgment of many people, the "natural" is the most obvious criterion of what is better or worse in sex. Natural acts are better in themselves, it is claimed, than those that are unnatural or perverted. The argument generally runs as follows: In the course of mammalian existence, sexual behavior has developed as a programmed mechanism for the propagation of the species. Though artificial insemination can also be used for purposes of reproduction, our sexual responsiveness has evolved as the normal means by which new generations can be produced. Natural sex is therefore sex that is heterosexual in the choice of an object, genital in the mode of expression, and coital in the service of orgasmic discharge. Although heterosexual, genital, and coital responses may be supplemented by other kinds of behavior, the latter can be considered sexual in a normative sense only if they are instrumental to or somehow derivative from the heterosexual, the genital, and the coital. If one lingers on peripheral activities, as in lengthy and possibly unconsummated foreplay, one is deviating from the natural. And if one chooses an object of the same sex, or seeks enjoyment that is not ultimately genital, as in scopophilia, or if one attains orgasm apart from coitus, the resulting conduct is inherently perverted and unnatural. Only when it serves the function for which it was "originally designed" can responsiveness be natural. Only in that context can one sex act be better than another, or good at all.

This approach sometimes leads to the assertion, by doctrinaire Catholics for example, that the reproductive mechanism is misused on *any* occasion when reproduction is not the implicit goal of sexual behavior. To be considered natural, and hence potentially good, sex must always be directed toward reproduction. Otherwise it can only be unnatural and lead to sexual perversions, the libidinal behavior having been misdirected toward ends that do not meet the preordained goals of species propagation.[10]

In all these beliefs, there lingers an ambiguity in the meaning of the term *natural*. As the word is ordinarily employed, it often refers to statistical regularities. And in this respect, one might very well speak of heterosexual coitus as the natural outlet for interpersonal sex as it now exists. If the human race were to reproduce itself primarily by means of test-tube babies, heterosexual coitus would become unnatural. That transformation of language occurs in Aldous Huxley's *Brave New World*. But any such use of words like *natural* and *unnatural* must not be confused with the sense in which something is natural if it involves the *appropriate* or *correct* adherence to what is given in nature.

The view that I have been summarizing declares, or just assumes, that heterosexual coitus is natural in both senses. That is why the term *perverted* is assigned to responses that do not fit the preferred pattern. Homosexuality or getting one's kicks by drinking out of a lady's slipper are called perversions because they are not reproductive and presumably entail a misapplication of the human syndrome that directly and indirectly furthers reproduction.

In opposition to this outlook, I suggest that it favors one of the facts of human nature but ignores others that are equally important. Our sexuality has evolved not only as a mechanism for propagation but also as an appetite that belongs to our need for interpersonal bonding. This need is in fact more fundamental than reproductive drive in the sense of being more characteristic of sexual situations as a whole. If we believe that statistical regularities should determine our ideas about the natural, I find no reason why interpersonal responses that have occurred through centuries of mammalian development should be downplayed or in any way subordinated. Only occasionally do people indulge in sexual behavior for the sake of reproduction, or at times that are optimally reproductive—for instance at midcycle, when a woman is most fertile. However minutely we analyze the appetitive

and interpersonal elements that are natural to our species
in either of the two senses to which I referred, we cannot
discover in these attributes anything that would prove
that "really" or in their "basic structure" they are
reducible to reproductive possibilities.

One might reply that if human sexuality were not
reproductive the species would not have survived. But
this does not mean that the reproductive function of sex
is more natural than any other. Nor does it imply that our
sexuality must or should be limited by its relevance to
species survival. Even if we think that evolutionary
processes and statistical frequencies prescribe what is
natural in the sense of suitable or appropriate behavior,
we misread the empirical data if we impart undue
significance to the reproductive element. Since that rarely
motivates sexual response, and is most often bypassed
completely, one cannot accept it as a universal criterion of
good sex.

Those who think reproduction has supreme importance
in the evaluation of sex do so because they believe it reveals
the purpose for which human beings have a sexual instinct
in the first place. As one might say that the biological
purpose of hunger is to assure that the cells and tissues of
the body are nourished, so too could one claim that
sexuality—above all, when it becomes an interpersonal
appetite—has the purpose of replenishing the species.

Notice that we have now shifted from function to
purpose in our description of the relationship between
sex and reproduction. This seems to me very crucial.
Once we realize the nature of this shift, we see that it
highlights the difference between appetites like hunger,
on the one hand, and sexual desire, on the other.

If we had the capacity to eliminate hunger without ever
nourishing the organism, we would say not that the

appetite finally has been satisfied, but rather that it has been eradicated. Imagine someone who took a drug that did nothing but suppress hunger. Feeling no urge to eat, this person might either waste away or else seek nourishment on the basis of wholly nonappetitive judgments. In that event, eating would not be a way of satisfying an appetite but only a means of staying alive. Eating would be like the act of looking both ways before you cross the street.

The same could be said of sex if the species were reproduced without sexual desire. People would use their genitals in a premeditative manner calculated to end in childbirth. Saint Augustine suggests that at first Adam and Eve had intercourse of that type. Since sexual desire resulted from the Fall, Augustine points out, Adam and Eve could have had no sexual appetite in the Garden of Eden. Presumably they were similar in their coital behavior to the person who does not feel hungry but knows enough to eat from time to time.

In the world that we inhabit, this analogy between sex and hunger fails. That becomes evident once we compare the two appetites more carefully. Except when it is being supplanted rather than satisfied, hunger does have the purpose of nourishing the organism. Hungry people may not give much thought to this fact; they may only attend to the discomfort in their stomach. But a biologist can rightly explain their eagerness to eat in terms of the nutritional pattern it manifests. For sex in relation to reproduction, there is no analogous explanation. Sex may eventuate in the birth of children, but when it does not it can be just as satisfying as when it does.

Or better yet, we might say that sexuality's biological purposes are more complex and more extensive in our being than those of hunger. By using sexual behavior to satisfy erotic, romantic, and libidinal (though possibly nonreproductive) inclinations, the organism is fulfilled in multiple ways that go beyond a simple appetite. Far from being constrained by anything like nourishment or the sustenance that nourishment provides, sexuality invigorates the body and expresses a wide gamut of feelings that enliven and augment one's entire being.

The human race survives not only by reproduction but also by social bonds that are needed for the healthy functioning of individuals as well as groups. The biological purposes that underlie our sexual behavior are more comprehensive than those that apply to either hunger or the desire to reproduce. Though a proper analogy might link these two urges, neither explicates the nature of sex. Hunger and the will to propagate may each pertain to an appetite of its own; but even if there is a reproductive appetite, this alone cannot elucidate the larger nexus of interpersonal relations that constitute the sexual.

There may, however, be another sense of *natural* that might yield a criterion for evaluation. Let us say that reproductive behavior entails a specific system of responses that people always experience as very satisfying. That would not be surprising, since evolution might well facilitate species continuance by making these instrumental activities extremely attractive. But, then, might it not be rational to recommend this way of life to people who—for whatever reason—may not know how enjoyable it can be? I think the answer is clearly yes. Nevertheless, this would not give us a new criterion of goodness. Though the satisfaction or enjoyment would result from engaging in reproductive activities, the criteria for evaluation would themselves be only satisfaction and enjoyment.

As a result, the most one could assert in this direction is that sex acts appointed by nature to encourage or promote reproduction often yield gratifications not found in other types of sexuality. It is conceivable that by and large, and throughout the entire population, these reproductive sex acts afford the greatest sexual satisfaction, whether or not they affect the rate of propagation. But plausible as this generalization may seem, it could be substantiated only by empirical research that no one has ever done.

One reason we lack the evidence that would allow us to rule on any such hypothesis is the fact that biology has not yet discovered which are the innate and programmed patterns of response that are required for reproduction to exist among human beings. If our sexual behavior were analyzable by reference to a biogrammar of instinctual motives, some of which are reproductive, we might be able to formulate ideas that would help resolve this difficulty. But given the present state of the life sciences, that conceptual development must still be quite remote.

5

Is There an Art of Sex?

Behind every evaluation that human beings make there lurks a recurrent question about the choice of criteria. Goodness or badness is always assigned on the basis of standards deemed relevant to the object or activity being evaluated. But who is to decide what these standards should be? Does not a decision presuppose a prior intuition of what is good or bad? And if so, is not our reasoning in such matters always circular?

The possibility that the logic of evaluation is indeed circular need not detain us here. Still we must realize that persons who evaluate differently may often have no way of reconciling through rational arguments the disparity in their choice of acceptable standards. In some cases disputes about criteria can be settled once all the facts are known; in other cases there may be buried inconsistencies that must be unearthed and exorcised. But frequently people evaluate the same act or object differently because they employ different standards and are wholly comfortable with their own.

We may all agree that in order for something to be good as an eating apple, rather than as a cooking apple, one must be able to bite into it easily. But if we have an apple that can be chewed with facility, must it be sweet or fairly tart, in order to be "a good apple"? Apple lovers do not all employ the same criterion, and there would appear to be no means by which evaluative disagreements of this type can be adjudicated. Instead we say there is a difference of taste, a difference of preference with respect to the goodness of apples, a difference of gustatory choice.

People sometimes claim they find it "hard to believe," "incredible," "amazing," that others should rely on whatever taste they have and use to justify their evaluations. But the giving of reasons for or against criteria one presupposes is normally not articulated. We may explain these differences by citing alternate determinants in individual physiology, and we do know that taste buds—for instance—vary in their operation from person to person and from period to period in a person's life. As long as someone is satisfied with his or her taste buds, however, and as long as he or she believes that they afford as much enjoyment as the taste buds that other people have, it seems irrational to suggest that this individual's taste is less reliable in the choice of evaluative criteria than anyone else's.

Even if we were sure that some tastes—for tart rather than sweetish apples, let us say—would give greater satisfaction to would-be apple lovers if only they had the taste buds needed to relish the tartness of an apple, those persons might still deny that this gives an adequate reason for them to employ criteria that are not grounded in their present taste. We cannot experiment with taste buds or change them at will, and we are not likely to say that what someone finds good in apples is not "really" good just because other people, with different taste buds, get (or seem to get) greater enjoyment from an apple of a different kind.

In some areas of life, our tastes and our preferences are more liable to modification than in the matter of gustatory quality. Our capacity to sense, to experience, and to recognize possibilities of goodness often lends itself to education or refinement. Much of moral judgment, most of aesthetic criticism, and almost all of what is called "art appreciation," is predicated upon assurance that the cultivation of recommended tastes is not only feasible but also justified in view of some eventual consummatory outcome. If people stubbornly refuse to improve their ability to like violin sonatas, we cannot condemn them as sonic idiots. That would mean imposing criteria that derive from a taste they do not have. But we can certainly say that appropriate evaluation of the goodness or badness of violin sonatas depends upon musical susceptibility related to that taste. It is always rational to demand suitable auditory taste as a prerequisite for crediting any evaluations of violin sonatas that someone cares to make.

I introduce these rudimentary thoughts in the logic of evaluation because they apply to questions about the goodness or badness of sex acts. I have been interpreting sexuality in human nature as a type of aesthetic experience that usually involves the body and the personality of other people in relation to oneself, rather than objects and events such as paintings or statues or performances in a theater. Lovemaking resembles the art of dance; and like other mixed media, it uses various sense modalities in a complex harmony that they establish with each other. Sex is a happening in which reality may mingle with illusion, spontaneous expressivity with the artificiality of contrived communication, emotional and sensate enjoyment with cognitive delight—all these combined through imagination and idealization as in any aesthetic project.

In arts such as music, painting, literature, and the dance, criteria of evaluation can often be legitimized by reference to the standards of some authority. Whether real or imagined, that person's judgments are taken to be exceptionally qualified for the specific art in question. We might say that these "qualified critics" are people who, in my previous example, have acquired a taste that is requisite for making trustworthy assessments of violin sonatas. Moreover, their taste is informed by a great deal of experience with music of this type, by a fairness in their attitude toward various productions in the art form, by an openness to new ways of enriching both the medium and their own ability to enjoy it, and by a significant amount of technical knowledge and detailed information essential for understanding how aesthetic opportunities it affords have entered into the lives of many human beings at different times of history. If such a person judges a violin sonata to be good, one has every reason to trust that judgment rather than the opinion of a man or woman who does not have similar qualifications. Is the situation at all comparable in the evaluation of sex acts?

From the outset, let us assume that sex is to be evaluated in terms of criteria that are pertinent to the interpersonal as well as the appetitive aspects of its being. We may then agree that anyone who cannot appreciate or enjoy sexuality as both an appetite and a search for bonding with another will be disqualified from making evaluations that we should accept as especially definitive. That person may have his or her own criteria; but we will discount them, as we would if someone who is hard of hearing and has no sense of pitch tried to evaluate violin sonatas. Nevertheless the question still remains: Can there be qualified critics for sex acts similar to whatever qualified critics we may recognize in the fine arts? If so, does this give us a means of preferring some or all of the sexual criteria I have been discussing? And if not, how should we settle matters in cases where different tastes cause people to choose one or another standard of what is good?

Initially it might seem strange to suggest that for sex as for art there may be qualified critics. We can surely imagine a Tovey or an Edmund Wilson or a Kenneth Clark being named a qualified critic for their respective media; we can even imagine someone (though there would always be much controversy about the person we choose) being called the world's *most* qualified critic in a branch of music, literature, or painting. But why believe that there can be anyone who is qualified to judge about sex with such magisterial supremacy? At the very least, it would be surprising to think that there might exist a critic more qualified in this area than everyone else throughout the world.

We tend to feel that way partly because sex has never been dignified as an aesthetic vehicle. As a consequence, we have hardly any tradition for the practice of criticism in relation to it. Also, sexual responses are more private and ephemeral than events in music or the drama, which can be preserved through written compositions; and unlike movements in the dance they are not amenable to rehearsals or a continuous method by which instructors can professionally impart standards of performance to later generations. It may be true that much of sexual behavior is learned through an apprenticeship, but this rarely occurs under the guidance of a master who is handing down accumulated know-how. Older women in the South Sea islands used to do something of the sort, and sex manuals obviously model themselves upon books that teach proficiency in the fine arts. For the most part, however, success or failure in sexuality is gauged not by the approval or disapproval of some seasoned veteran but only by the extent to which the participants themselves are satisfied by their own mode of improvisation.

As against this idea that sex does not conduce to the existence of qualified critics, it might be said that Freud, or Kinsey, or contemporary sex therapists, would be the equivalent. But even if we could reach agreement about the preeminent status of these authorities, why should they be considered uniquely qualified *as critics*? Their attainments being what they are, one might only classify them as scientific or medical experts. They may also be superlative counselors. But to be a "sex critic," if I may coin the phrase, similar to people we call music critics, literary critics, dance critics, and so on, someone would have to possess a vast amount of personal experience, a long history of diversified sexual behavior, much knowledge about human nature as well as erotic techniques, wisdom about the vicissitudes of affective attachments, and, of course, the good sense needed to make credible judgments that affect the intimate lives of other men and women.

People of this type do exist, but we may ask whether they alone are qualified to judge the goodness or badness of any sex act. There is something in the character of our sexuality that distinguishes it from the traditional art forms. To put the problem tentatively, as an approximation, we might say that the aesthetics of sex depends upon the occurrence of idiosyncratic impulses in a manner that music, literature, painting, and the rest do not. I will try to clarify this statement presently, but first I want to suggest that the great variability of sex makes it impossible for any individual—a Don Juan, a Casanova, or even a highly proficient sex therapist—to be *as* qualified in this region of life as many critics are in the other arts.

Sex has this limitation because there is no single or uniform structure that functions alike in all of sexuality. Even though sex is always founded on one or another pattern of instinctual response, people are tremendously different in their sexual feeling and behavior. The fine arts do not have an identical structure either, but they are relatively abstract and sex is not. Hearing mellifluous sounds and looking at lively images may be instinctive, but the appreciation of music and painting is much more than that. As the products of technical training, their constructions are all cultivated artifacts. They are alterations and refinements—what I elsewhere call "transformations"—of everyday experience. Each is the florescence of a highly intensive learning process.[1]

Sexual response, too, includes attitudes or gestures that are often learned and not innate, and these may also require the acquisition of a special aptitude. But sexuality is unlike any other art in one respect. There is an unmistakable drive toward sex that virtually all human beings recognize, and frequently feel very strongly throughout long periods of their maturity. Nothing comparable to this applies to the fine arts. Although music or painting or literature fills the existence of many people, so totally sometimes that their need for these modes of expression takes on the vital importance that sexuality has for most other men and women, and for themselves at various moments, sex differs in being available to everyone and throughout his or her experience.

Beethoven was a person in whom the appetite for music was probably greater than his sexual appetite. If he were representative of the human race, we might conclude that his creative impulses—cerebral and usually noninterpersonal—are more indicative of human instinct than the responses of people whose craving for sex vastly exceeds his. As things are, however, Beethoven is a rarity, a glorious and exceptional sport of nature. In most human beings, sexual desire arises spontaneously and without a prior search for its creative possibilities. All people can perform sexually without schooling or special genius. For that reason, anyone in general may rightly insist that the instinctual drive he or she personally experiences is a more reliable guide to good sex than pronouncements that some connoisseurs might offer as a testament of what they themselves feel. For this reason alone, sex and its criteria for goodness are always more relativistic than other art forms.

At the same time, one could say that even satisfied lovers can benefit from instruction about methods of enhancing sexual enjoyment. Not everyone is able to give good advice, and there are practices that we may not even be aware of until we have been encouraged to try them. That requires sophistication about sexual techniques, and insight into their hedonic potential. If someone has both the requisite talent and the acquired knowledge, is not that person outstanding in this field? Possibly so. People who have these advanced credentials may be well qualified to make helpful suggestions. And yet, expertise in the evaluation of sex can never be the same as it is in the fine arts.

For one thing, an art critic is not thought to be qualified unless he or she has had a wide experience in the medium. But the situation is different in relation to sex. Couples who remain strictly monogamous may fail to garner the joys that come from promiscuity, spouse-swapping, furtive adultery, and orgiastic abandon; but we would not want to say that they cannot be fully qualified to judge the goodness or badness of their own sex acts. That possibility arises only if people express distress and somehow indicate that their sex life has been unsatisfying. An utterance to this effect might make us wonder whether they are missing out on something and could profit, perhaps, from more liberated experience. But it is also possible that, in their case, the quality of sex falls short for psychological reasons that would not be altered by enlarged experimentation. If an unhappy man or woman finds a preferable lifestyle that can abolish the bad memories of earlier events, everything might change for the better. There is, however, no way of knowing that beforehand.

When the sexual behavior of a monogamous person is very satisfying to him or her, we are inclined to believe that this individual is just as qualified to evaluate sex acts as the connoisseur who has had a more adventuresome erotic life. I am not suggesting that promiscuous men or women are *less* qualified. That would imply that something in the nature of monogamy or pair bonding makes it intrinsically preferable to promiscuity. An assumption of this sort is as indefensible as the idea that promiscuity is in itself better than pair bonding. Each has its own advantages and disadvantages.

The delights afforded by promiscuity are obvious, but possibly detrimental to the attainment of interpersonal and appetitive satisfactions that human beings also cherish and that only nonpromiscuous behavior can enable a man or woman to enjoy. For its part, monogamy can become boring: by definition, it excludes extramarital enjoyment. Even so, monogamous people are not less qualified as evaluators of the sexuality they have chosen for themselves than someone who sleeps with many others and tries everything sexual under the sun. The idea of there being a uniquely qualified sex critic is therefore highly dubious.

One might argue that in no art is there a qualified critic whose judgments cannot be contradicted by other qualified critics. And if this is correct, as I believe, we could infer that the relativity of sexual taste resembles the disparity of authoritative judgment in the fine arts. Being so thoroughly dependent upon the artificial devices of their particular media, however, the fine arts require a level of preparation and concerted training that goes far beyond primal nature. The same cannot be said of sex. Though it is also an aesthetic pursuit, sex is closer to our biological being. More than any other art form, it is—in the words of the show tune—"doing what comes *naturally*." The proficiency that involves puts sexuality in a class of its own.

Conclusion

Toward a Theory of Sex

In offering these reflections about the nature of sexual response and whatever criteria might be relevant to its evaluation, I have systematically ignored problems about the morality or immorality of sex. In our species, as it currently exists on this planet, sexuality is a fact of life. To ask whether sex is good as a moral entity would seem to be like asking whether life is ethical. But what sense can it make to ask whether existence, or being alive, is morally better in itself than nonexistence and not being alive? Better to whom, and by what objective standard?

These questions boggle even the metaphysical mind. Certainly we do and must make inquiries about the ethical status of particular acts or events or experiences *within* life. Under some circumstances it would be wrong, morally reprehensible, to give preference to one's own desire to exist if that means sacrificing the legitimate claims of many other people who also want to stay alive. But to ask whether any human beings ought to exist, in general and apart from the effect upon nonhuman creatures, has little or no meaning—at least, not to me.

Similarly, I find it very hard to imagine what could recommend either a positive or a negative ethical judgment about sex as a generic whole.

Those who feel the need for such judgments do so, I believe, because they have become alienated from their natural state. Having found that sexuality in themselves, and in other persons, is not as benign or satisfying as they had hoped, they wonder whether its mere occurrence is morally justifiable. To say it is not is to imply that one perceives some alternative possibility that may warrant our approbation. What could it be? A utopia in which people no longer feel the affective impulses, needs, organic urgencies that characterize humanity at present? Once again, we are drawn back to the brave new world of Huxley's science fiction. But that world, brave or hideous as we may deem it, is not our world.

Those who are in touch with ours, and who have thought about the being that nature has instilled in us, may feel that it is useless to ask about the morality of sex in its totality. Sufficiently at home with the responses it makes available to them as individuals, they are concerned only about the moral implications of satisfying sexual demands through one or another option. Their ethical questioning pertains to the sexuality they contemplate as a viable possibility for themselves and others. In that regard, ethics is always secondary. And yet its application to sex is utterly essential if we are to live a good life. Approached from that vantage point, the problematic morality of sex takes on great importance.

This assertion may seem paradoxical. In my previous chapter, discussing the art of sex in relation to art forms such as painting, music, literature, and the others, I proffered the idea that sexuality is in itself aesthetic. Should we not treat its ethical aspects in a comparable fashion? What I have just written would seem to rule that out. I reply by noting that ethics and aesthetics are different in their logical structure. Speculating about sexuality as an art, I tried to see whether this might show us how we should employ the evaluative criteria that are internally relevant to it. The ethical import of sex is something else, and quite distinct. It pertains to what I have been calling "external considerations."

Far from telling us what sexuality is in itself, ethics deals with our need to adjudicate the consequences that our sex acts might have for some other creature. The "ought" or "ought not" of this deliberation is normative in that respect, and it plays a principal role in all our purposive activities. Wanton sexual conduct can do a great deal of harm both to us and to everyone else involved. Our pluralism must never be allowed to conceal the moral dangers that forever lurk in any sexual endeavor.

These dangers, like the benefits that may accrue once we learn how to surmount them, issue from the fact that we are imperfect beings who seek not only what is good but also what is better. Ethics is an operative element in this quest, and in that sense an intimate companion of aesthetics. But the ethical cannot alter the basic character of sexual phenomena. It affects them, but only by selecting among them. To this extent, sex resembles all the other arts. Though ugliness, in a painting as in life, may not be aesthetic, no ugliness—whether graphically portrayed or present to interpersonal experience—can be inherently either moral or immoral. It is what it is: a candidate for aesthetic evaluation that we may consider ethically good or bad not because of what *it* is but solely in its impact upon those who are affected by it. That is true of sex in all its modalities.

I labor this distinction between the aesthetic and the ethical because so many people think of sex in moralistic terms. Their greatest spokesman is Kant. Unswervingly and with much analytical acuteness, he articulates the underpinnings of the sexual morality he inherited from his Lutheran origins (and beyond in Christian orthodoxy). As Luther had proclaimed that human depravity causes every appetite or self-fulfillment to be sinful in itself, so too does Kant argue that sex is intrinsically immoral. Being an attempt to enjoy another person for reasons of one's own, it seemed to him a selfish and appetitive appropriation of another person. Consequently, it inevitably impedes our desire, if we are moral, to treat that person *as* a person, as a unique and autonomous end in him- or herself. Sexuality as such is unethical, Kant believed, because it is, by its very nature, inimical to the respect that every human being deserves.[1]

Kant presents this conception as a stepping-stone that leads on to his idea of marriage as the prerequisite of sexual love. Through the marital relation, he says, one overcomes the immorality of sex by submerging it within a contractual agreement predicated upon the mutual and reciprocal love of one's spouse as just the person he or she is. The details of Kant's argument I can bypass in this place. Here I wish to focus on his having founded the ideal of sexual love upon the alleged worthlessness and even immorality of sex as it exists apart from its reconstitution in marriage. That is what I consider most harmful in his view.[2]

Apart from difficulties in Kant's suggestions about the nature of matrimony, the nature of personhood, the nature of love, and the nature of ethics in general, his philosophy assumes a viciousness in human sexuality that is prejudicial to an understanding of it. By treating sex as nothing but an appetite, Kant ignores its interpersonal component as well as its ability to enclose within itself a significant form of love and compassion. Far from supplanting the appetitiveness of sex, marriage at its best validates and actively cultivates this natural inclination by means of the positive and interpersonal bonding that may accompany it. Hume, who also believed in the goodness of marriage, thought that sex is a life-enhancing instinct wholly compatible with loving-kindness and the search for beauty. Compared to Hume's approach, Kant's claim that marriage is needed to cleanse the evil of sexuality appears ignorant and barbaric.

Roger Scruton's ideas about sex are interesting in this context because they avoid some of Kant's misconception about the nature of matrimony while also supporting the Kantian notion that apart from the morality inherent in marriage sexuality must be ethically suspect. On the one hand, Scruton states that "The value of marriage lies in . . . the fulfilling of [sexual desire]. Marriage creates thereby the objective conditions for the genesis of desire."[3] But Scruton does not make this statement in order to assert that marriage is a valid goal or haven for sexual desire, but rather because he believes that without the sanction entailed by the moral institution of marriage sex would not be intrinsically good. Scruton claims that "there could be neither arousal, nor desire, nor the pleasures that pertain to them, without the presence, in the very heart of these responses, of the moral scruples which limit them."[4] On his view marriage is the appointed means of satisfying those scruples.

Though this does not imply that sexuality is immoral in itself, it reinstates Kant's belief that sex has no inherent goodness. As I have been arguing, this is a mistake that an acceptable theory of sex must guard against. Human sexuality always has the potentiality of being moral, if only as something that conduces to happiness for ourselves and others.

The possible morality of sex is guaranteed by its internal relation to both love and compassion, as well as its capacity to satisfy each participating person in ways that are not injurious to anyone. Neither love nor compassion is necessarily ethical, since they can be misused or delusory or such as to eventuate in action that is hurtful rather than humane. Although love and compassion are not extraneous to sex, the morality of their involvement must always depend on the practical circumstances in which they themselves occur. But when they are indeed ethical, their expression through sexuality of any type will also be ethical.

While my presentation in this book skirts many important questions in sexual ethics, some of the moral implications of what I have said should be mentioned in this place. I list them without much elaboration and mainly in anticipation of future work:

1. Society should recognize and acknowledge that the criteria we have discussed can represent legitimate standards that individuals have a right to accept or reject as they wish. Political and judicial authorities have a correlative obligation not to hamper the pursuit of any relevant experience and behavior, or to mandate a preferential status for one or another criterion that they might personally choose.

2. Even if there were general agreement that the maximum satisfaction of all criteria would be ideal in some society, each person should be allowed to decide for him- or herself how the criteria will be organized in

relation to each other and in accordance with the different sacrifices that are required for someone to effect a viable harmonization. No ideal, however grand and ennobling it may seem, should be allowed to preclude every possible divergency from it.

3. All means of satisfying one's sexual urges should be considered equally moral, equally permissible, provided that they entail no harm to anyone else. Correspondingly, those who engage in deviant ways of satisying their own criteria of goodness must not be punished or deprived of their rights of free expression unless their activities do in fact harm others.

4. Nevertheless, society has an undeniable obligation to protect minors against sexual molestation, and the same applies as well to adults who have or would have withheld their free consent in relation to activities abhorrent to them.

5. Difficult cases are sure to arise from the possible conflict between 3. and 4. above. For instance, should society regulate, perhaps banish, obscene or pornographic films and magazines on the grounds that such material is offensive to many people? Should teachers whose sexual orientation is unrepresentative in some way be excluded from their profession because they do not serve as role models in the society to which their pupils belong? Do parents have an obligation, or even a right, to encourage the development of one or another type of sexuality in their growing children? There is no univocal answer to these questions, at least none that is universally acceptable on the grounds of ethics alone. But in saying that, I am only reminding the reader that sexual morality warrants investigation beyond the limits of this book.

❄

Other issues have also been ignored or barely treated in the theory I have sketched. Though my distinction between the sensuous and the passionate may be helpful in itself, a thorough examination of its role within a more detailed conception of sex seems indicated. I hope that my critics and commentators will find a way of using the distinction to their own advantage and from their own point of view. That, as the saying goes, is something only time can tell.

My distinction between the libidinal, the erotic, and the romantic resides in a similar state of limbo. When I first introduced that distinction, it abetted my pluralistic rejection of essentialism by showing that sexual love includes these very different kinds of response. With its emphasis upon the genital and reproductive elements of sex, the libidinal had been given excessive prominence by Freud and many other theorists. I wanted to call attention to the greater, in fact all-pervading, presence of what I called the erotic. Describing it as a gravitational tug that draws us into the affective orbit of persons, things, ideals, and even ourselves, I maintained that the erotic—unlike the libidinal—is primarily an aesthetic phenomenon. Though I was reverting to Plato's idea of Eros as a motivational force in nature, I felt that I was exploring terra incognita and that the elusiveness of the erotic might itself explain my inability to analyze it as fully as I would like. The romantic seemed more manageable, since it embodies interpersonal bestowal and the search for a permanent love of some particular person, both of which are conditions I had already examined at length.

As I argue in this book, all three of the coordinates in that distinction occur within the parameters of mere sexuality, sex without love, as well as sexual love. But an extended theorization of sex is still needed to elucidate the mutually interwoven roles of the libidinal, the erotic, and the romantic in the affective life of human beings. Here, too, much more work must yet be done.

Three further challenges should also be acknowledged in this concluding statement. About two of them I have written quite a lot in other places; about the third, scarcely anything. The reader may have noticed that in my comments about hedonic criteria for sexual evaluation, I refer a few times to "consummation." It is a term that some philosophers have substituted for *satisfaction* or *enjoyment*. Since a sizable chapter of my book *Feeling and Imagination: The Vibrant Flux of Our Existence* is devoted to consummation as a goal of all human affect, I could have addressed the nature and evaluation of sex from that perspective. In *Feeling and Imagination* I project the ordinary usage of *consummation* into regions of life that are often only remotely related to sex. I attempt to show that various social and even cosmic feelings may be consummations of our being even though they are not overtly sexual and might not at all be reducible to sex.[5]

But in that book my speculation sometimes has an aura of intuition, and even oracular surmise, that I accepted as unavoidable in view of the ideas I was struggling to express. Discussing criteria of sexual goodness in the book you have now been reading, I decided that the more common, and in some ways more precise, terminology of Western hedonism would be preferable. Sexual consummation overlaps enjoyment as well as satisfaction. I thought that these terms would suffice as a reference to its hedonic quality and its place among criteria of sexual goodness. Since I was giving the outlines of a theory specifically about sex, I felt that my broader ideas about consummation might well be left in their own conceptual domain—at least, for the time being.

Throughout my writing, I have also grappled with the need to find a more complete understanding of the nature of imagination than philosophy has been able to attain as yet. I made imagination central to my analyses of love, and in several places I mentioned its function in human sexuality. Those reflections lie just beneath the surface of what I have been saying here. But the fascinating relation between sex and imagination demands much more analysis than anyone has undertaken thus far.

The other concept that I shortchange in the current book is the notion of pansexualism. It is a view that Sartre seems to espouse at several points, and I have occasionally acknowledged the possibility that it may follow from certain implications of my thought as well. If one sees the erotic as having a universality in our affective attachments comparable to the pull of gravity in the material world, one is presupposing that sex permeates all human existence. I am not troubled by that assumption. As long as we recognize that we are talking about the erotic ingredient of sex, and not its libidinal or romantic components, I am willing to countenance the possible truth of the pansexual theory. Like all metaphysical beliefs, it is not verifiable. But that does not deter me.

At the same time, I doubt that the pansexualist concept can do much work in my philosophy. It is a generalization about sex rather than being a part of its definition. In the order of beliefs that matter to me, it does not rank very high. I find it comforting and mildly erotic in itself, but as a theorist I can live without this article of faith. The operative meaning it has for me is rather limited.

For others it has had enormous importance. I know it weighs heavily in the writings of Henry Miller, D. H. Lawrence, and the Marquis de Sade. But few philosophers, or creative writers in general, have given it as much credence as they do. Are the pansexualists pathological in their persistent affirmation, or are they courageous and unwavering as devotees of a naturalistic religion that merits our respect? I remain undecided. Here, as in much of my life as a thinker, I am willing to suspend both belief and disbelief.

Notes

Preface

1. For a useful survey of recent feminist, post-Freudian psychoanalytic, social constructionist, and "queer" theories of sex, see Joseph Bristow, *Sexuality* (London: Routledge, 1997), including a bibliography. See also Vern Bullough, *Science in the Bedroom*: *A History of Sex Research* (New York: Basic, 1994); and Igor Primoratz, ed., *Human Sexuality* (Aldershot, England: Ashgate, 1997).

2. Together with the books listed in note 1, chapter 1, see two books by Alan Soble: *Sexual Investigations* (New York: New York University Press, 1996) and *The Philosophy of Sex and Love: An Introduction* (St. Paul: Paragon, 1997); both include good bibliographies.

Chapter 1: Sex, Love, Compassion

1. See in particular the following anthologies: Alan Soble, ed., *Sex, Love, and Friendship: Studies of the Society for the Philosophy of Sex and Love, 1977–1992* (Amsterdam: Rodopi, 1997); Robert M. Stewart, ed., *Philosophical Perspectives on Sex*

& *Love* (New York: Oxford University Press, 1995); Alan Soble, ed., *The Philosophy of Sex: Contemporary Readings*, 1st ed. (Totowa, N.J.: Rowman & Littlefield, 1980), 2nd ed. (Savage, Md.: Rowman & Littlefield, 1991), 3rd ed. (Lanham, Md.: Rowman & Littlefield, 1997); Robert Baker and Frederick Elliston, ed., *Philosophy and Sex*, 1st ed. (Buffalo: Prometheus, 1975), 2nd ed. (Buffalo: Prometheus, 1984); Robert B. Baker, Kathleen J. Wininger, and Frederick A. Elliston, ed., *Philosophy and Sex*, 3rd ed. (Amherst, N.Y.: Prometheus, 2000). See also Igor Primoratz, *Ethics and Sex* (London: Routledge, 1999); and Jennifer Harding, *Sex Acts: Practices of Femininity and Masculinity* (London: Sage, 1998).

2. Irving Singer, *The Pursuit of Love* (Baltimore: Johns Hopkins University Press, 1994), 51–72.

Chapter 2: Patterns of the Sensuous and the Passionate

This chapter is partly based on material, now revised, in my book *The Goals of Human Sexuality* (New York: Norton, 1973).

1. Saint Jerome, *Against Jovinian*.

2. Milan Kundera, *The Unbearable Lightness of Being* (New York: Harper & Row, 1984), 246.

3. Quoted in Countess of Blessington, *Journal of the Conversations of Lord Byron* (1834), 317.

4. Lycurgus, quoted in Denis de Rougemont, *Love in the Western World* (New York: Anchor Books, 1957), 50.

5. Sigmund Freud, "The Most Prevalent Form of Degradation in Erotic Life," in *Sexuality and the Psychology of Love* (New York: Collier Books, 1963), 67; alternate translation in *The Standard Edition of the Complete Psychological Works of Sigmund Freud* (London: Hogarth Press and The Institute of Psycho-Analysis, 1957), 11:187–88. Freud's complete works are hereafter referred to as *SE*.

6. Freud, *SE*, 11:180.

7. Freud, *SE*, 11:181.

8. I have discussed this at much greater length in my chapters on Freud in volumes 1 and 3 of *The Nature of Love*. See

Irving Singer, *The Nature of Love: Plato to Luther* (Chicago: University of Chicago Press, 1984), 23–38; *The Nature of Love: The Modern World* (Chicago: University of Chicago Press, 1987), 97–158.

9. Stendhal, *On Love* (New York: Grosset & Dunlap, 1967), 2.

10. Stendhal, *On Love*, 3.

11. Stendhal, *On Love*, 5.

12. A. W. Watts, *Nature, Man, and Woman* (New York: Mentor Books, 1958), 167.

13. W. H. Masters and V. E. Johnson, *Human Sexual Inadequacy* (Boston: Little, Brown, 1970), 309.

14. Act 1.

15. Theodor Reik, *Love and Lust* (New York: Farrar, Straus & Giroux, 1957), 190.

16. See *The Nature of Love: Plato to Luther*, 7ff; *The Nature of Love: The Modern World*, 383–90.

17. On all this, see volumes 2 and 3 of my love trilogy: *The Nature of Love: Courtly and Romantic* (Chicago: University of Chicago Press, 1984), passim; and *The Nature of Love: The Modern World*, passim. See also my book *The Pursuit of Love*, 125–76.

Chapter 3: The Nature and Evaluation of Sex

1. Arthur Schopenhauer, *The World as Will and Representation*, trans. E. F. J. Payne (New York: Dover, 1966), 2:533.

2. In chapter 5 and the conclusion, in which I contrast the aesthetic and the ethical dimensions of sex, I return to the idea that moral (and therefore social or political) considerations are external to the inherent nature of sexuality.

Chapter 4: Criteria of Sexual Goodness

1. See Gilbert Ryle, "Pleasure," in his *Collected Papers* (New York: Barnes & Noble, 1971), particularly 326–28.

2. On this, see my book *The Goals of Human Sexuality*, 26, 66–82, and passim.

3. See Thomas Nagel, "Sexual Perversion," in his *Mortal Questions* (Cambridge: Cambridge University Press, 1979), 39–52. See also Soble, *The Philosophy of Sex and Love*, 165–78.

4. Sara Ruddick, "Better Sex," in *Philosophy and Sex*, ed. Baker and Elliston, 1984, 280–99.

5. For further discussion, see two essays by Robert C. Solomon: "Sex and Perversion," in *Philosophy and Sex*, ed. Baker and Elliston, 1979, 268–87; and "Sexual Paradigms," in *Philosophy of Sex*, ed. Soble, 1991, 39–62. See also Russell Vannoy, "Philosophy and Sex," in *Human Sexuality: An Encyclopedia*, ed. Vern L. Bullough and Bonnie Bullough (New York: Garland, 1994), 442–49.

6. Ludwig Wittgenstein, *Zettel*, 2d ed., ed. G. E. M. Anscombe and G. H. von Wright, trans. G. E. M. Anscombe (Oxford: Blackwell, 1981), 88. Wittgenstein's remark: "Love is not a feeling. Love is put to the test, pain not. One does not say: 'That was not true pain, or it would not have gone off so quickly'" (#504).

7. See *The Nature of Love: Plato to Luther*, 3–22 and passim; *The Nature of Love: The Modern World*, 390–406; and my rejoinder "A Reply to My Critics and Friendly Commentators," in *The Nature and Pursuit of Love: The Philosophy of Irving Singer*, ed. David Goicoechea (Amherst, N.Y.: Prometheus, 1995), 323–61, particularly 325ff.

8. See also İlham Dilman, *Love and Human Separateness* (Oxford: Blackwell, 1987), 74–92. For a contrasting view, see Russell Vannoy, *Sex without Love: A Philosophical Exploration* (Buffalo: Prometheus, 1980), 7–29.

9. Jean-Paul Sartre, *Being and Nothingness: An Essay in Phenomenological Ontology*, trans. Hazel E. Barnes (New York: Philosophical Library, 1956), 389, and 282–406 in general; Maurice Merleau-Ponty, *The Phenomenology of Perception*, trans. Colin Smith (London: Routledge, 1996), 167.

10. On this, see G. E. M. Anscombe, "You Can Have Sex without Children: Christianity and the New Offer," in *Ethics*,

Religion, and Politics, The Collected Philosophical Papers of G. E. M. Anscombe (Minneapolis: University of Minnesota Press, 1981), 3:82–96. See also the following in Baker and Elliston, ed., *Philosophy and Sex*, 1984: Pope Paul VI, "Humanae Vitae," 167–84; and Carl Cohen, "Sex, Birth Control, and Human Life," 185–99. For a more general discussion of views about natural and unnatural in sex, see Soble, *The Philosophy of Sex and Love*, 27–38.

Chapter 5: Is There an Art of Sex?

1. I employ this concept in several contexts but develop it most fully in my book on cinematic transformation: *Reality Transformed: Film as Meaning and Technique* (Cambridge, Mass.: MIT Press, 1998).

Conclusion: Toward a Theory of Sex

1. See Immanuel Kant, *Lectures on Ethics*, trans. Louis Infield (New York: Harper & Row, 1963), 162–69.

2. For further discussion of Kant on sex, love, and marriage, see two chapters in my book *Explorations in Love and Sex* (Lanham, Md.: Rowman & Littlefield, 2001): "The Morality of Sex: Contra Kant" and "The Morality of Compassion: Contra Kant and Schopenhauer." See also *The Nature of Love: Courtly and Romantic*, 377–93 and passim.

3. Roger Scruton, *Sexual Desire: A Moral Philosophy of the Erotic* (New York: Free Press, 1986), 360.

4. Scruton, *Sexual Desire*, 362.

5. On this, see *Feeling and Imagination: The Vibrant Flux of Our Existence* (Lanham, Md.: Rowman & Littlefield, 2001), 95–141 and passim.

Index

About the Author

Irving Singer is the author of many books, including *Feeling and Imagination: The Vibrant Flux of Our Existence*; *George Santayana, Literary Philosopher*; *Reality Transformed: Film as Meaning and Technique*; and his trilogies, *Meaning in Life* and *The Nature of Love*. He is a professor of philosophy at the Massachusetts Institute of Technology.